ENDORSEMENTS

In Goodbye Lies. Hello Life. *Jodi Goshorn shares her own journey of healing and deliverance by exposing some of the most common lies and strongholds in a believer's life. But more than simply telling her story, she provides insights into why these lies emerge and offers practical wisdom in how to defeat their deadly sting. She offers strategic scriptures that reveal God's truth concerning the strongholds, as well as detailed prayers to help the reader demolish these lies and walk in the truth. Her illustrations are raw and honest, and will not only stir hope and promise, but give readers some great spiritual tools in saying goodbye to the lies and hello to a new life in Christ.*

Wanda Alger,
Ordained Minister, Author, and Speaker

Goodbye Lies. Hello Life. *by Jodi Goshorn hits many valuable points. First, it is a short and quick-read. And it was encouraging and to-the-point of the message. From beginning to end, Jodi develops the purpose of heart, the challenges of the lies we can accept, the way of escape, and the truth to get there. Each chapter is stand alone and diverse in its intention. The reading is easy and the pondering is enlightening. Whether just becoming a Christian and desiring to deepen your walk, or having served in the Kingdom for 47 years, there's something to touch your heart in what she expresses and has learned in her Life. I highly recommend Goodbye, Lies. Hello Life. to all who pick it up. Prepare to be challenged!*

Dr Robert B. Kisner Phd.,
Mercy University
Brian Kisner Outreach

I value the stories Jodi tells and how they reveal her earnest search for God. She invites the reader into this process, illustrating how Scripture helps to orient her view of God and her view of herself. I also appreciate how Jodi creatively presents a series of Truth Darts that help to organize and translate the Bible passages for our modern ears. I recommend this book as a devotional text, study material for a class or small group, or an invitation to a seeker.

Paul J. Yoder,
Teacher Education Professor,
Eastern Mennonite University;
Chair of the VMMissions Board of Directors

Jodi writes with refreshing vulnerability, spiritual depth, and gentle authority. Throughout this life-giving book, she guides readers through a healing journey from hidden lies to deep inner freedom, offering a blend of personal story, biblical truth, and practical steps.

What makes Jodi's voice unique is her authenticity. She doesn't write from a platform, but from a life rooted in communion with God. Her words carry compassion, wisdom, and the power to help others encounter Jesus face-to-face.

This book is more than encouragement; it's an invitation to transformation, and Jodi is a trustworthy guide for the journey.

Rob Stoppard
Author, Speaker, and Consultant

goodbye
LIES
hello
LIFE

Uprooting the Subtle Deceptions

Keeping You from Abundance

jodi goshorn

TABLE OF CONTENTS

"It's easier to pretend I don't believe lies than to uncover the truth and deal with them."

"Being like Jesus seems unrealistic and unattainable. God can't possibly expect me to be like Jesus here and now."

"I don't need to cut ties with my painful past or work at releasing unforgiveness to receive inner healing."

"I am loved based on my own good deeds."

I dedicate this book to my six children:

Levi, Julia, Aden, Aaron, Samuel, and Elim. You've been present throughout much of my journey—and consequently experienced my sorrows and joys—firsthand. It is my hope that by uprooting the subtle deceptions, your lives will also be forever impacted for good and for His glory, as Jesus reflects through you. I love each of you and pray for you: "to know the love of Christ which surpasses knowledge, that you may be filled to all the fullness of God." (Ephesians 3:19)

FOREWORD

As Jodi's father, it's such an honor to introduce you to the daughter I raised and know so well—a woman who is secure in her identity in Christ, and who is filled with unconditional love for herself and others.

In this book, Jodi speaks honestly about her own experience—how the weights of adulthood were placed on her at a young age, and consequently led to her feeling the need to live up to the expectations of others. She took courageous steps to uproot the lies that could have kept her in bondage for a lifetime. This book will guide you through these strategic steps, and hopefully lead you to those encounters with Jesus which are crucial for shifting your thinking and boldly walking in truth towards total freedom.

I found myself captivated by the confidence my daughter exudes with the turn of each page of this book. I hope you will be encouraged as you read about Jodi's journey through these challenges, and find yourself equipped with the tools to adjust your mindset as you walk through your own trials with resilience and confidence. Jodi's prayer and desire is that this book would help to liberate each reader to be uniquely who they were created to be!

Benjamin R. Musser,
father

INTRODUCTION

Are you undone by Jesus's kind interactions with others, such as welcoming the wayward woman who poured oil at His feet and stooping low to heal the man born blind? Does His compassion captivate your heart? Do you marvel at His miracles, like feeding the five thousand with just five loaves and two fish? And are you ever overcome, with eyes brimming, *by how intensely Jesus loves and cares for you?*

Maybe. Or maybe not—at least not in full. It could be that your own interactions with Him are shallower and more infrequent than you'd like—than He would like. Maybe your obedience to God has gained you friends and followers but left you feeling hollow, and powerless inside. Although you want to be impactful for His kingdom, something is holding you back. Rather than feeling exhilarated, your faith has grown comfortable and complacent. And you're frustrated. Because, even though you say all the right words and do the good and godly things, you're not experiencing the life Jesus promised—not really.

The thing is, God wants every person to apprehend abundant life even more than we can imagine! His sacrifice freed us from sin, but this truth is not a quick fix. Although Christians believe in Jesus, *many neglect digging deep enough to uproot the lies that hinder them from encountering Him in everyday life*. The subtle deceptions distort their perceptions and become filters that shape paradigms and, through individuals to groups, affect the whole world.

If abundant life is not your reality, then lies are likely holding your faith, too. They could be causing you to partner with the very thief that Jesus said would come to steal and kill and destroy. (John 10:10) But I'm sure you picked up this book because you want to encounter Jesus more intimately. So, just keep reading, my friend!

The Path That Leads to Life

Ignorance kept me from apprehending the full freedom Jesus made available. Due to emotional trauma, relational dynamics, and church hurt, I fell prey to the lies presented by the enemy. I built walls to protect myself, but I only trapped myself inside them. Although my obedience to God appeased my conscience, I was painfully stuck managing unnecessary symptoms.

Specifically, the lies I believed were an assault on my God-given identity and resulted in anxious and guarded timidity. Although I wanted to do great things for God and His kingdom, my lack of self-belief caused me to remain a shy and quiet

Christian. Shame hindered me from the abundant life I dreamed of, and many afternoons I lay broken on my bedroom floor, tears streaming down my face. Reaching desperation, I finally faced my fears and courageously cried out, "*God, why do I feel like I'm just not enough for You?*"

Looking into His loving eyes, I realized how intensely He cared for me and desired to commune with me. He wanted to restore all the missing pieces inside, to heal me. His love empowered me to trust Him and surrender my whole heart to His profound Holy Spirit. As I invited Him to remain near He began to "search me and know me" on the inside. He already knew it all—the good, the bad, and the ugly. And He wanted me to know it too. With my faith as permission, He revealed the places in me where lies had taken root and patiently pointed out where I needed freedom.

As I applied myself to the work of forgiveness, to replacing the lies with truth, and to meditating on His Word, He rewrote my looping mental "tape." Through a consistent lifestyle of authentic heart-to-heart conversations with God, He gave life to my soul!

In truth, I am a regular person. I don't hold any particular ministry roles or titles, though I love Jesus with my whole heart and have come to know Him intimately. I enjoy being a wife and mother and praying for our growing family, and larger community. My big heart reaches wide and supports those near and far. Of course, I still make mistakes—I am human. But my perspective is no longer shaped by shame or tainted by the lies I once believed. And now, because Jesus removed the yoke of a people-pleasing spirit, I am free to share my God-story with you.

Our life experiences may be similar, or very different. But regardless, somewhere along the way, we have all made agreements with the accuser. And there is hope for your freedom, for living a powerful, fruitful, and fulfilling life here and now! Why? Because He did it for me—a regular Christian. He is faithful, and all things really do "work together for good to those who love God, to those who are called according to His purpose." (Romans 8:28)

Destructive lies sound simple enough to detect, and yet they're sneaky. Our perception is easily distorted. You might wonder, *What are practical first steps, and where do I begin to uncover such lies?* Don't worry, think of the plan in this book—where I share helpful, discovered landmarks—like a guiding GPS. I've experienced emotional healing from painful traumas by proactively replacing lies with truth, and God wants all of us to experience the glory that comes from "stripping off every unnecessary weight and the sin which so easily and cleverly entangles." (Hebrews 12:1 AMP)

At the outset, I introduce our collective problem and where the lies come from. Then, throughout the course of the book, I detail how lies shape our identity, sharing pertinent and inspiring details from my story. My inner conversations that led to truth encounters with Jesus are italicized for easy identification. Next, I'll lead you through the process of replacing the lies with truth. Each chapter that emphasizes a particular lie also contains a "Communion" section, which will provide opportunities for you to intentionally meet face-to-face with Jesus. Then, as a response, there will be a short "Prayer for Healing." Since "the word of God is living and active, and sharper than any two-edged sword," these chapters also close with "Truth Darts." (Hebrews 4:12) They are bullet-point scripture passages to read as declarations. Refer to each of these sections frequently and definitely apply them in everyday life! (Please note: Reading this book does not discount the need for getting professional help. If your case requires it, do not neglect seeking a trained coach or therapist.)

Freedom through Truth Encounters

Freedom to be the person God intended is possible! Fears caused by false perceptions will fall away as you learn to rest in your God-given identity as His well-loved child. As the Holy Spirit leads you to replace lies with truth, He will bless you with new, healthy habits. Then, the capacity to carry His presence will increase and the fruit of His Holy Spirit will grow within. And deeper peace and patience with yourself and those around you will also mature. Abiding in Him will become the new normal. Allowing His words to transform you will embolden your faith, as rivers of living water flow from within—just as Jesus promised! (John 7:38)

As individuals grow in Christ, the whole body of Christ will also heal and mature! We will stand more firmly upon the foundation of Jesus Christ, outgrowing our old, restrictive patterns and paradigms. Spiritually and emotionally healthy, we will create strong communities capable of sustaining His kingdom among us. And just like "cities on a hill," (Matthew 5:14) these cultures will shine bright, revealing His glory as we fellowship with Him and each other. Wholly free sons and daughters will effectively minister God's heart, mystically shifting the atmosphere of Earth and consequently setting all of creation free from bondage. With natural grace, God's people will appropriate His authority and govern according to His mandate, as He imagined. And, together, we'll encounter the fulfillment of Jesus's prayer, "Your kingdom come. Your will be done, on earth as it is in heaven." (Matthew 6:10)

What about you? "Are you tired? Worn out? Burned out on religion?" Jesus encourages all of us, "Come to me. Get away with me and you'll recover your life. I'll show you how to take a real rest. Walk with me and work with me—watch how I do it. Learn the unforced rhythms of grace. I won't lay anything heavy or ill-fitting on you. Keep company with me and you'll learn to live freely and lightly." (Matthew 11:28-30 MSG)

The path ahead has been prepared; and He is

the Way! It's through an intimate knowledge of Him that we are set free. (John 8:32) Remember, it was Jesus Himself who said, "I came so they can have real and eternal life, more and better life than they ever dreamed of." (John 10:10 MSG)

My greatest hope is that this book will help you identify and dismantle deep-rooted, oppressive lies and empower you to take steps towards creating consistent truth encounters, for abundant life everyday!

CHAPTER 1

ABUNDANT LIFE: ROADBLOCKS

Every year after Thanksgiving, my strong sons carry the heavy storage bins of treasured Christmas decorations up the stairs from the basement. We crank up the holiday tunes and carefully remove the contents from the bins. While sipping hot cocoa, we reminisce about Christmases passed.

One year, when I opened the lid and dug into the collection of our precious keepsakes, a stench stung my senses. Finely nibbled shavings trailed from the plastic bag of salt-dough ornaments we made years before when the children were young. Other items were ruined too. Eventually, I noticed the tiny hole in the corner of the bin where the small critter had bitten through and escaped from, leaving lots of damage behind.

Just like a mouse in a stored Christmas bin, we often aren't aware of the mess inside our hearts until we open up and look inside. The truth is, Jesus already accomplished everything necessary to set us free from sin and shame. All too often, though, Christians don't experience the full freedom he granted for us on the cross. And why is that? The Bible teaches us that we have an adversary, for whom we are to "be on the alert," because the devil is prowling around "like a roaring lion, seeking someone to devour." (I Peter 5:8)

While giving the devil too much credit for our messes is dangerous, so is denying the reality of the enemy that seeks to kill, steal, and destroy all that God loves. Believing in Jesus doesn't mean we're automatically immune to the devil's attacks. *Who me? I'm a Christian; I don't believe the enemy's lies*, we tell ourselves. But, by our indifference towards his tactics, we actually disregard our real authority over him—our spiritual muscles grow weak. In effect, neglecting to address areas of darkness within us makes us especially susceptible to their serious consequences.

From scripture, we understand the enemy is "the accuser of the brethren." (Revelation 12:10) So, anytime we define our reality based on his lies, our view of God, ourselves, and others becomes skewed. Throughout this book we'll specifically look into some of the lies that attack our identity in Christ, and their resulting foul consequences.

Where the Lies Come From

Because lies are subtle, most people don't understand their origin or their effects until they intentionally search. Just like the Christmas-bin mouse from years ago ruined many family treasures, so undealt-with lies fester and cause trouble for individuals and even whole families. They wreak havoc until the lies are exposed.

Did you know that 95% of our decisions are made subconsciously? Though our brains are constantly perceiving, thinking, feeling, and deciding, only a portion occurs within the realm of awareness—which means that only 5% of our brains are being utilized on a conscious level. And this is important, because humans are often tempted to trust everything they see and feel, and thus fall into the enemy's trap by inadvertently agreeing with his twisted version of stories. Lies take root through past experiences and interpretations of them. A basic study in human psychology reveals how our hearts and minds are most pliable during childhood. Based on one article, "Decades of research in developmental psychology, pediatrics, and neuroscience have converged on the conclusion that the first five years are especially critical. During these years, children begin to explore their environment, learn verbal and reasoning skills, socialize with others, and, eventually, take steps toward asserting independence from their family."[1]

---

1   https://www.psychologytoday.com/us/basics/child-development

And so, core memories during early developmental childhood years impact our whole lives. Painful memories—of fear, trauma, and unhealthy interactions—can lead to deep wounds, especially when the circumstances are recurring. Likely, shame entered because we felt alone; and our enemy took advantage of our pain. There, in the weakest and most vulnerable moments, many people believed false narratives and made agreements with our accuser. The lies took root and became the foundation for future beliefs.

The Seriousness of the Issue

Although the enemy's version of our stories is not true, his lies are believable to many. Sadly, even Christians have normalized the resulting mental and emotional struggles, and the unhealthy relational dynamics. Before Jesus set me free from the enemy's lies, I thought I wasn't worthy to receive God's love. When I messed up, I believed He was displeased with me. And fearing His rejection, I distanced myself emotionally. Eventually, it led me to try harder—to *be more* and *do more*—to earn acceptance from God and others.

Like I was, many believers are stuck in cycles of fear and shame, bound to managing unnecessary symptoms. This is a brief introduction to a few of the common lies Christians are tempted to believe and will be unpacked in the following chapters.

Many believers are often naive to the lies that trap them and assume their systems are normal, *just the way things are.* They rationalize that *everyone else is struggling too* so don't dig deep enough to uncover the truth of who they're meant to be in Christ. Or because they don't believe they are uniquely valuable—worthy of God's love even—they settle into a false sense of security. Some wonder how Jesus' life has anything to do with theirs. And since their experiences are so far removed from His, they disconnect themselves completely. *Jesus's abundant life is just too good to be true for me.* They might even believe their own experiences more than scripture. And their faith might lack real purpose. Instead of pursuing God's best, they settle into mediocrity. Seeking the truth requires effort, and so some have become lazy. Rather than cleaning up their messes, they allow the negative cycle of consequences to continue. Year after year the lies pile up. And just like a fusty Christmas bin left on the shelf, the mess gets worse.

Lies create dysfunction within families, communities, and church cultures. And just as they affect individual lives and relationships, lies also set forth judgments that affect the whole Earth. By misunderstanding our corporate identity as God's holy and beloved people, many Christians misunderstand our collective purpose, too. (Colossians 3:12) As sons and daughters of God, we are mandated to govern our earthly sphere according to Heaven's order. But we've fallen short of this glory and handed our authority over to the enemy, instead. Living according to lies allows for global chaos through paradigms that are not aligned with God's best. And, in fact, "the whole creation groans and suffers the pains of childbirth together until now." (Romans 8:21-22)

Choosing Intimate Encounters

While pain from the past isn't our fault, taking responsibility for the resultant mental mess is. Though lies may begin small, they fester and multiply if not dealt with. But just like the Christmas bin, if we're intentional, we will know when something isn't right inside our hearts. And through purposeful pursuit, the culprit can be uncovered.

How can we deal with lies that are lodged in our psyche? Consider this: Jesus said true life is found by knowing the Father. (John 17:3) And as a human, He knew God. He intimately encountered the Father and made the way for us to encounter Him too! Following Jesus's lead, we must learn to commune with the Holy Spirit. To ask the deep and often difficult questions, and then wait—patiently—for His heartfelt answers. *Why do I do what I do, God? Where are the broken pieces hiding in my subconscious memory? God, would You reveal the lies so that I can be truly free?* And this is how to encounter Him—in truth. "For now we see in a mirror dimly, but then face to face; now I know in part, but then I will know fully, just as I also have been fully known." (I Corinthians 13:12)

The Father longs for His creation to behold Him, and to feel His love and acceptance. By leaning into His kindness, the broken places are exposed, so they can be healed. In knowing Him intimately, we can become whole and naturally reflect *His* glory!

By clearing out the ruined decorations from the Christmas bin, space was made for new ones. In the same way, God leads His children to take the bin from the shelf, and address the clutter of the enemy's lies—since He wants each one to experience the greatness that comes by "stripping off every unnecessary weight and the sin which so easily and cleverly entangles us." (Hebrews 12:1 AMP) Inner healing comes through intimate truth-filled encounters with the Word—as the Holy Spirit reveals the power of the living Jesus.

Together we'll consider a few specific identity-lies Christians hold onto that hinder them from experiencing the abundant life of His glory. We'll discuss how believing the lies negatively impacts individuals and also stifles the whole body of Christ. As wisdom is imparted, you will be led into personal truth-filled encounters. And His love will lead you to surrender your whole heart to His profound Holy Spirit's inner work. So that by identifying lies, you will be empowered to pull them out by the root and replant the truth of His living Word.

Intimate Encounters

COMMUNION

The "Communion" sections are moments to encounter Him face-to-face, to receive His loving embrace. Just like the father received the prodigal son who returned home, our heavenly Father longs to welcome you into His embrace and bless you with His peace. Breathe in deeply. Allow yourself time to intimately connect with the Father in communion, as you'll be "strengthened with power through His Spirit in the inner self." And He'll reveal "the width and length and height and depth, and to know the love of Christ which surpasses knowledge, that you may be filled to all the fullness of God." (Ephesians 3:16-19)

Communion is purposefully placed before the "Prayer for Healing" section, because through these encounters with Him, you will become empowered to respond. He loved us first, so we can love Him back.

PRAYER FOR HEALING

Healing comes by honest assessment and an intentional choice to return to the Father. And so, the "Prayer for Healing" sections of each of the following chapters are opportunities for you to come before God in repentance. In this case, repentance is simply "the heartfelt return to a face-to-face connection with the Father." Do not fear, for there is no shame in His eyes. And so I encourage you not to rush through the prayers. For healing doesn't come by words alone, but rather through the humbled heart of a well-loved child.

And by this, God will reveal the truth of His Word, "And you will know the truth, and the truth will set you free." (John 8:32)

Truth Darts

At the end of each chapter, there are declarations called Truth Darts. They are meant to be a prophetic activation and are provided to aim directly at the lies uncovered during the chapter. Our words are important and carry power, so by using your voice to speak God's living and active Word, you are indeed proclaiming your submitted agreement with Him. Speak the truth aloud to set a new course in your heart and mind. Take time with them. Meditate on them. Repeat the scriptures over yourself throughout your everyday moments. Dog-ear the pages and refer back to them often.

Again, speaking scripture out loud is powerful!

Finding Freedom Requires Courage

Why sabotage God's best by settling for old, worn-out belief systems, especially since real and abundant life has been bought and paid for by Jesus?

Just as the disastrous damage done by the mouse wasn't visible on the outside of the Christmas box, no one can imagine the profundity of the lies we believe until serious inventory is made. That Christmas bin was foul, and many items were ruined. But what if my family had not taken it down and looked inside? Even more precious pieces could have been ruined than were. In the same way, without intentional digging, freedom can't be fully discovered.

While it's never easy uncovering pain, accessing the life dreamed of with God requires authenticity when addressing some difficult questions. Healing takes courage. Dear friend, I am praying for you to discover the joy that comes by intimately encountering His truth!

CHAPTER 2

MY STORY

For a long time, I maintained privacy in order to protect my pride and preserve my reputation. But that helped no one. The truth is, we all have both positive and negative memories from our past—childhood is like that. And we remember according to our limited knowledge. Even children raised within the same family hold varying opinions of a particular memory. Just ask my brother! And so, although these memories I share may not be accurate according to others' views (or possibly even my own if I'd experienced them at a different phase of maturity), these accounts are written from my personal lived experience. And that is exactly the point: how we remember our past shapes our beliefs, and therefore our self-held identity. Maybe you can relate?

Many good things transpired in my young life—and I am grateful—but the emotional environment surrounding my early childhood also became the seedbed for rooting lies within me. My parents dearly loved my brother and me, and I only recently realized just how blessed I was. Ours was a simple life in a small town. My parents were married young. They were in love, and I was born two years later. Dad built our beautiful house in the country, on a plot of land from the farm he was raised on, and my grandparents lived next door. Many days I dropped into Grandma's kitchen for chats and special treats.

On warm afternoons in the spring, my brother and I played in the backyard or went on adventures around the pond until dinner. The songs of newly hatched peepers drifted in from my open bedroom window at night, and I used to lie awake and soak in all the simple sounds and smells of spring. My family talked and laughed as we took long walks on Sundays after church; and we prayed together, too. We played but worked even harder. During summertime, Saturdays were for pulling weeds from the garden or picking berries from the bushes Dad had planted. We splashed each other with the garden hose as we washed the car. And on crisp autumn evenings, we raked leaves in the backyard before jumping in the huge piles. Winter treks and sledding trips down nearby mountain roads are also happy memories forever frozen inside my heart. Seasons changed, and the years whizzed by.

Dad was successful as a young businessman, and always very busy. Phone calls with clients and subcontractors filled his days. In the evenings, he sat at the small drop-leaf table in our kitchen with his pen and yellow legal pad, where he wrote out long to-do lists. I learned to not interrupt him when he was working, lest we be shushed for being too rowdy. I don't remember ever climbing up onto his lap or telling him silly stories. Dad wasn't unkind, just seemingly uninterested.

Mom was usually busy, too. I didn't ask her about boys or relationships, though. Mostly, she seemed emotionally unavailable for intimate conversations that were important to me. I could always tell when she was angry about something, as she busied herself deep-cleaning a room or organizing a closet or drawer somewhere. When we made messes or didn't complete tasks to her standard, she scolded my brother and me. And when she was in "one of her moods," I tried to steer clear. I kept to myself or read books in my bedroom. *Best to be seen and not heard* became my inner motto.

Dad and Mom argued frequently and sometimes loudly when I was little. During their conflicts, Dad talked more, and Mom withdrew, usually giving us the silent treatment. Sometimes, the emotional distance seemed to last for days. Though I felt emotionally detached, I tried to please them. Desperately, I offered my thoughts, though they ended up sounding childish and unimportant, invalid even. And I often questioned my value. *Does my voice matter at all*?

The Lies I Believed

Although I knew I was loved, I didn't feel emotionally safe or connected. This inner rollercoaster was wildly unpredictable and created such sadness and anxiety. *Can I be vulnerable with my feelings and still be accepted*? I hoped so—but wasn't brave enough to keep practicing when I felt rejected time after time. I learned to protect myself by staying out of the way and keeping quiet. My feelings seemed dangerous. Wary of their value, I opted to stuff them inside. The enemy took advantage of my innocence and whispered lies, *You are weak and powerless. You'll never carry any real authority in life.* And I fell victim to the untruths.

Over time, my role became to look pretty and please the adults in my life. When I measured up to their expectations, I received their attention. When I didn't, I felt emotionally ignored. And so, looking good, being good, and doing good became a thick, heavy blanket that eventually smothered me. I believed my value was tied to pleasing others, and my goal was performance. Yet, no matter how hard I tried, nothing seemed good enough. I couldn't measure up to the standards set by others—or those put on myself. And this sting of shame kept me trapped in performance mode, painfully striving.

Though I knew there was so much more inside me, no one seemed interested. Deep thoughts and feelings swirled. I longed to feel seen and known—and nurtured—as my imperfect self.

But, our family hosted church picnics and New Year's Eve parties. My parents led home groups and were the youth group leaders. To others, we were the family that "had it all together," and I couldn't reveal my hidden secret: *we weren't perfect, and we didn't have it all together.* While I didn't want to be alone, I believed I couldn't show my imperfections, and so the hope for being truly known and loved seemed beyond my reach.

The insecurities I learned from my family's relationship dynamics instigated an inner struggle for me socially, too. Though I longed for real and healthy friendships, I was so scared to be authentically myself. Vulnerability seemed too risky, even dangerous. And I believed another lie: *There's no one to share myself with. I'm alone.* Fear distanced me, and conflict was extremely uncomfortable. Interacting with people different from myself seemed impossible, since I equated disagreement with rejection. And I judged others by the same cloudy lens through which I saw myself. People seemed flawed and forever needing to be "fixed." There was little joy in simply being myself or allowing others that same freedom. Though I appeared strong, stable, and sure of myself on the outside, I was actually scared, stiff, and stoic. Still, I dreamed of walking in the freedom of being myself.

Growing Up With God

With gratitude, I honor the heritage of my godly upbringing, for it led me to Jesus. Even as a young girl, I connected deeply with God and felt his love for me. I heard Him speaking directly to me, and I knew He was close.

Before bed each night, Daddy read us Bible stories as tears trailed down the sides of his cheeks. Jesus came alive to me, and I wanted to know Him. When I was eight years old, my parents led me to kneel at our living room sofa and invite Jesus to come into my heart. From then, I knew He was always with me. My dear grandmother taught me to bring my burdens to Jesus in prayer, and she nurtured my faith in Him. In those early years, I experienced His simple and strong love as my safe place. He gave me the courage to forgive and trust that everything would be okay, somehow. With Him, there was no pressure to perform.

Beautiful pink sunset skies on summer evenings reminded me of His affection. Music brought me to tears as I sensed Him near, joyfully singing my made-up love songs back to Him. I'd naturally converse with Jesus, my friend. Unashamedly, I loved Him with all my heart and devoted my future to Him. I trusted God had a purpose for my life; I only ever wanted to please Him and love others like He did.

My relationship with God grew, and my faith matured. As a young woman, receiving prophetic words through trusted friends became a more common occurrence. I felt truly seen by God. Those prophetic words were like secret promises, on which I pondered deeply. They gave me hope.

Excitedly, I dreamed of what God would accomplish through my life, our adventure together!

I began planning for a life of service, pursuing what I believed was most valuable to God. Little by little, though, the same weight of performance for authority figures placed a wedge between Him and me. Slowly, it became more difficult to feel close. Of course I loved Him and desperately wanted to please Him, but my service strayed into what good act I could do for God rather than simply being with Him, as myself. The fear-based stress followed me, *Is He proud of me? How can I make my life count for Him?* I wondered. *Doing work* for the Lord became most important.

For me, ministry was an ambiguous list of roles considered most valuable. Being "called into ministry" felt like receiving a confirmation of His special favor, and so I equated ministry titles with signs of being chosen. Not only that, the ones called by God seemed to carry more spiritual authority. Those "called into ministry" seemed to possess an obvious edge, as if they were more important.

While I knew God's love was real and true, over time I began caring more for the accolades and admiration of others. I didn't dare appear face-to-face with Him, for fear He'd see my faults. His inner Voice of Truth became dull and more distant, and so I defaulted to doing what I thought looked good and godly. Receiving acceptance was a vicious cycle that became like a noose around my neck. Over time, it felt like I was "on-duty" and "being a good example" rather than simply treasuring a real relationship with Him. I forgot about His pure, strong love, and I missed being myself with Him. Without ever realizing it consciously, I became distracted by my "calling."

Marriage

Within the church culture I was raised, standing out or appearing showy was not looked on favorably, since it gave the impression of being proud. Women, especially, were supposed to be quiet and reserved, or so it seemed. The men were strong and outgoing, natural born leaders of the home. When I read, "The husband is the head of the wife," (Ephesians 5:23) I interpreted it as, *No matter his personality, the man is expected to boldly lead the family—in every single situation.* I believed that *the man is the more powerful partner who carries the spiritual authority, while the wife is supposed to remain quietly submissive, carrying none.*

Randy and I met and fell in love during high school. From the very beginning of our dating relationship, I put parameters on myself to "simmer down" and expected him to display the boldness that I wanted to live out but believed I shouldn't. While each of us loved Jesus for most of our lives and knew we wanted to serve God together, our personalities diverged from the traditional norms that I thought should be present within a godly marriage.

Throughout our early years, I compared

myself to the quiet Christian women in my life, whose personalities and callings were different from my own, and Randy with the men in celebrated leadership roles. *What is wrong with me?* I questioned. *Why did God create me with such ambitious dreams when women are supposed to stay quietly submissive?* And Randy was also brought under the heavy, scrutinizing pressure of my fierce judgment: *Why isn't he acting like the bold authoritarian leader he's supposed to be?* I felt incredibly frustrated with my situation. Because I was more focused on outward appearances and believed identity lies, I misunderstood the abundant life Christ was offering. Equating humility with living small and powerless, I stuffed my passionate personality and shied away from expressing myself outwardly. I piled on layer after layer, and eventually got lost inside them.

Moving Across the Globe

Together, Randy and I believed we were called by God to do overseas missionary work. Happy dreams filled our young, naive hearts, and on a cold January morning in 2006, we carted an excessive amount of luggage to the airport. Together with our almost two-year-old, smart and soft-hearted son, and our tiny, nine-month-old lovable baby girl, who even then became the adventurous traveler she still is, we moved across the globe. Rubber touched down late at night in muggy Bangkok, where an estimated seven million people surged throughout the bustling city.

Thrilled to become part of a church-planting team in Thailand, we settled into life among a least-reached people group.

While we had grand ideas of sharing Jesus with the people of rural, northeastern Thailand, God used this time to adjust our own perspectives of what real ministry actually is. At some point during the nearly seven years we were there, I lost hope of ever realizing the grand "ministry" visions I had for my life. *Is my life's work even meaningful at all?* I wondered. Friends and teammates were busy visiting remote villages, telling Bible stories in Thai, and doing important things for God. As a busy wife and mother of four young children, I felt isolated and incredibly lonely. *What am I even doing here? How is my life making any difference?*

I saw some fruit in my efforts to pray for people while my children played at the park, and I experienced some fulfillment trying to talk with strangers at coffee shops. But generally, I was tired and troubled. I did not feel like I was adventuring through life with God. *Maybe I didn't hear Him, and perhaps I'm not actually "called into ministry" like I thought.*

My Matryoshka Doll Moment

Life-altering moments happen when we're least prepared for them.

We had been in Thailand for four years, and our team met for a mini-retreat. A short-term prayer team was visiting from Pennsylvania. There I was, sitting expectantly on the cold tile floor in the middle of the living room, awaiting my turn for some encouragement. *Now would be a perfect time for another prophetic word from You, God.*

And then, one of the women started speaking to me. She saw me as covered by complex layers, like Russian nesting dolls masking the smaller doll inside. Stunned, I felt angry, cheated by God, even. "What do you mean by complex layers?" Somehow the word felt embarrassing, like the word "layers" revealed the shameful proof I wasn't good enough. There it was, all out in the open—exposing me. I felt raw and betrayed. Maybe the others had seen what I hadn't. That I needed fixing, to be and do better, so I could measure up and make God proud.

For a moment I begged the excuse, *But, I've experienced culture shock and felt homesick for my family. I've praised You even through the difficulties here, God. What more do you want from me?* Then, I blame-shifted. These *people from America are supposed to be praying for me, encouraging me in the good works I'm doing for God. Shouldn't they be seeing all the amazing things He's doing in my life?*

I felt numb. And my heart had become hidden. Lost, even from me. All the subconscious fears and insecurities I had buried down bubbled up. Even though I had been a Christian for most of my life, junk had piled up around my soul and was hindering me from experiencing the full, abundant life of Jesus. And at that moment, I knew. Something had to change, and it wasn't my circumstances or the people in my life; it was me. Over the next weeks and months, the Father continued to pursue deeper places in my heart. He provided opportunities for me to encounter Him face-to-face, and to uncover what was inside me. I was impelled to deal with the difficult questions in my heart, so the lies could be exposed and the layers peeled back. For He designed to emerge and heal the real *me*.

Through the process of replacing the lies with His truth, the Father faithfully revealed my true identity in Him, not merely as a servant but as His beloved daughter, and as an heiress to the throne, just like Jesus. Little by little, wholeness became more important than appearing "put together," and *my best for His glory* became my mantra.

By taking time to commune with Him and to learn His voice, I encountered the tenderness of Jesus, and He reminded me that His yoke is comfortable and His burden is light. (Matthew 11:30) As I learned to rest in Him, He empowered me to let go of unnecessary rules and regulations, the systems and approaches I had misunderstood as the crux of Christian life. I released every good and godly goal that God hadn't ordained for me. And, as I applied His Word to my everyday life experiences, His promises became real!

In the same way Jesus had just *one mission*, that is all He required of me—to remain in Him. (John 5:30, John 15:4) Just as the smallest matryoshka doll loses all her outer layers, I had been undone. Jesus helped me remove the heavy weight of expectations that were never meant for me. And now, I'm consistently becoming the secure, confident, powerful, and loving child I thought I couldn't be, the person He always intended for.

Your Story

Every person has a story; some drastic and others mostly regular. Ours could be similar or perhaps very different—though equally important. Some Christians seem to "have it all together," and even lead others to put their faith in Jesus, though they may not experience His glory for themselves. Not wholly, anyway. Though they love God deeply, they still don't feel close to Him, and they desperately want to. The Father seems distant or uninterested. They've tried fixing themselves, to *be and do better*, so they can measure up and make God proud. Something is out of order, though. And their identity is lost somewhere inside their piled-on layers.

Like them, maybe you picked up this book and whispered, "Now would be a perfect time for another prophetic word from You, God." But uncover lies? *I thought this would encourage me in all the good deeds I'm doing for God.* And in the same way I felt angry on the cold tile living room floor in that faraway place, even cheated by God, you could be tempted to write me off. *She doesn't know my story.* And you'd be right. Though I'm not certain about the details of your journey, I realize their value, especially to Jesus. In fact, the freedom from lies, and the peace and joy—it's all about Him!

Just like the man born blind that Jesus healed said, "one thing I do know, that though I was blind, now I see," (John 9:25) I have nothing more to offer beyond what He offered me. Draw near, friend. I am confident that as you courageously commune with His Holy Spirit, your intimate encounters will lead you into all truth.

CHAPTER 3

I'M FINE. IT'S FINE. EVERYTHING IS FINE.

"It's easier to pretend I don't believe lies than to uncover the truth and deal with them."

Recently I hosted a small gathering of women who met regularly to pray. As we sat around the table at a local coffee shop, sipping our espressos and listening for nudges from the Holy Spirit, heartfelt tears began to stream down my face. If you know me, tears are my response to His near presence.

When we closed our prayer time and finished the last of our lattes, my friend leaned in close and gently pointed out that, as a result of my—now dried—tears, large black mascara rings were left under my eyes. "I didn't think you'd want to go on not knowing they were there," she giggled. The thought of going about my day looking like a raccoon was funny yet embarrassing. Her honesty blessed me greatly! Because she loves me, she spoke the truth and allowed me to remedy my ridiculous situation. I dabbed hard as I repeatedly questioned her, "Did I get it all, yet?"

I could have become frustrated with myself for not wearing waterproof mascara. Or, ignoring her because I didn't see the residual rings around my eyes, I could have denied the messiness altogether. Maybe they aren't really there. But neither of these options would have changed the craziness of my circumstance.

The Lie Explained

Saying we don't believe lies is similar to pretending we're not wearing mascara rings. We don't know what we don't know. Ignorance is most detrimental to our inner life—gravely worse than simply looking ridiculous. The problem is that lies won't just go away on their own. Mascara rings aren't removed without careful attention. And similarly, refusing to look honestly at our beliefs bars many Christians from the abundant life Jesus promised. Internal lies about who God is and who we are in Him are more pervasive than could be imagined. So, whether or not we realize yet, lies are the culprit which clogs capacity to receive God; and they block us from flowing in His abundance.

Some people are naturally bent towards introspection and self-awareness. They detect their own faults and blame themselves more easily than others—berating themselves for imperfections instead of putting energy into seeking helpful solutions. And often they allow the enemy to further antagonize their mind by believing they deserve to feel ashamed. These lies may have even become the sounds of their inner voice.

Others are less self-aware. Their fear of experiencing pain is greater than the desire to confess, make amends, or correct their ways. So they'd rather ignore the pain than face the hurting parts. Acknowledging the truth hurts, and so they tend to take flight instead. While their lives look fine enough on the outside, they may be spiritually lukewarm and neglect becoming all that God created them for. Often people who think like this are unaware of how their attitudes and actions negatively affect others. Things definitely aren't fine.

And still, others are simply stubborn and deny the truth altogether. *Nothing is wrong with me; it's everyone around me who needs to get their act together.* Pride has overtaken their inner lives. Appearing as if they "have it all together" has become their prize. But, denial is deadly. For the enemy lies in wait of our destruction. Therefore, each of us must give careful attention to our beliefs. There is always a reason for not experiencing God's overflowing abundance in our daily lives—and we must be willing to search that out.

Truth from God's Word

When we're presented with the truth, we have opportunities; and the truth is that God has not authored the lies we believe. His enemy tempted the first humans to agree with him, and he continues in the same vein with each of us today. The story opens like this:

> *"So God created man in His own image, in the image of God He created him; male and female He created them. God blessed them; and God said to them, 'Be fruitful and multiply, and fill the earth, and subdue it; and rule over the fish of the sea and over the birds of the sky and over every living thing that moves on the earth.'"* (Genesis 1:27-28)

God placed Adam and Eve within a perfect paradise, naked and unashamed. That blissful Garden of Eden was their home, where God walked and interacted with them in close, unbroken fellowship. He designed them to experience vulnerable, loving interaction with each other as well. His purpose for them was to spread and enjoy governing their earthly home according to His design. But the cunning serpent tempted and won over Eve, "Eat the fruit; you don't need God. You can do as you please and still experience life, apart from Him. He's hiding something, withholding life's pleasures from you." Our enemy has not changed his line since.

Their purpose is our purpose, too! But since that first day, by our agreements made with the very same enemy, sin has released its slow, sad fade within the human race. Often, we think of sin as "things that appear wrong by human standards." But, understanding sin in this way sets us up to miss the deeper truth. In reality, by allowing even seemingly small untruths to invade space inside our hearts, we are led to ruin. And that, my friend, is where sin begins: falling short of the glorious life He destined for us in Christ. By our own fear, we have turned away and become enslaved. Like sheep, all of us "have gone astray." (Isaiah 53:6)

Consequences for Disregarding the Truth

By refusing to admit we've made agreements with the enemy, we further sabotage our freedom. Pretending that "everything is fine," when it obviously isn't, only perpetuates our problems. Lying to ourselves is like being wrapped up in pride, and it leads us down a path towards death and destruction. "If we say that we have no sin, we are deceiving ourselves… If we say that we have not sinned, we make Him a liar and His word is not in us." (1 John 1:8, 10)

Individuals who struggle knowing their own faults all too well, often allow their shame to separate them even further from God. Just as the first humans doubted, others may also wonder if He is as good as He says He is. They might even question, "Did God really say…?" and not really believe the truth that "nothing can ever separate them from His love." (Genesis 3:1, Romans 8:38-39) Or, some Christians turn away when they fail, because they fear He'll reject them—but nothing could be more untrue! Even though He will never turn away, some believers are stuck in fear. And so, they grant doubt a space inside their minds and fall further into mistrust of who God is and who He says they are. They may even mimic the lies of the enemy, enter into twisted agreements, and fall prey to unbelief. *God can't really be that good of a Father. He is hiding something from me and won't deliver what He promised.* Just like Eve, they might turn away. *I don't really need to be close to God. I can experience a good enough life apart from Him.*

Still, other Christians choose to cover up the lies that lead to death. And they deny believing them at all. Rather than confess unbelief, they neglect the sin that has entangled their hearts and minds. But, when they hide in their shame, the spiritual problem leads to emotional—and sometimes even physical—decay. Every area of their lives becomes tainted, and the unhealthy patterns not only hurt themselves, but also others they love. But, covering up rather than cleaning up authorizes the enemy's foothold and allows sin's slow death to continue its work. Therefore, be encouraged to get rid of "every obstacle and the sin which so easily entangles." (Hebrews 12:1)

The way was made! And we desperately need the Holy Spirit: to reveal the path of life and lead us into all truth. (John 16:3) Sadly, some Christians settle, and choose to appear acceptable rather than actually submit to the freeing discipline of our loving Father. But thinking we're exempt from the consequences of sin actually closes us off to His remedy. And by denying that we believe lies, we shun His gift and actually separate ourselves from His grace.

The Path to Life

God always sees and knows, and He lovingly calls us out. Even when we feel lost, He reveals the way through our intimate connection with Him. And as we consistently allow Him, the Holy Spirit faithfully exposes the lies. And then we must actively participate with Him and apply His truth to every out-of-order area He highlights. He shines the light, not to condemn but to reveal truth! Even though it doesn't always feel good, His near and loving presence brings comfort. (Psalm 139:23-24)

Until I looked fully into Jesus's fiery gaze, I couldn't receive His love and forgiveness. But when I became willing to trust Him enough to let it all go—the good, the bad, and the ugly—that's when I encountered Him. In reality, my honest confession wasn't for Him. It was for me! It was necessary for my healing. (1 John 1:9) Perhaps He is saying to you as He did to me, "Dear child, remember the layers. The process of uncovering them and being bare before Me is for the cleansing of your conscience; both conscious and subconscious memories. Are you willing to come clean for your own good?" In truth, God doesn't want you just pretending to be fine. He actually wants you to become more than fine—to be healed, whole, and set free.

Dear friend, none of us were ever meant to live in mediocrity or hindered by the enemy's lies, not even slightly! As we look into some specific lies that even Christians are tempted to believe, remember this: Jesus said we would find Him when we seek Him with all our heart. (Jeremiah 29:13)

Ultimately, His blood settled the debt for all time, and His great sacrifice opened the way back to the Garden, where it all began. But only intimate knowledge of the truth will set us free. Although freedom is available, we must be willing to bare it all to Him. Each person must become truthful with our inner selves and with God. And we must allow His Holy Spirit to search us and truly know us. Even if pieces of our hearts and minds became broken and perhaps even lost to our subconscious, God sees and knows. He's always aware, and He loves even better than we could ever love ourselves. We can trust Him to care for us and lead us into all truth. Like a faithful Father, He will always receive us. His discipline is for our healing, so that we may be set free from the inside out.

Intimate Encounters

COMMUNION

"Dear Child, I am here and I have always loved you. I have not authored the lies you believe but have opened the way ahead by the precious blood of Jesus's sacrifice. Along this journey I will expose the lies, not to hurt you but to cleanse your conscience. By following in the Way of Jesus, you will know the path. My Holy Spirit will shine the light as long as you allow Him. Stay close, and He will comfort you. The truth is, nothing can separate you from Me. Release your fears of not being enough and your shame of having fallen short. I will restore all that has been lost and stolen. I work all things together for good, because I am good."

PRAYER FOR HEALING

"Father God, I acknowledge You have never led me astray. Thank You for continuing to pursue me and expose the lies I believe, so that I can lay everything before You and be healed. I realize I have made agreements with the enemy. I trust that Your grace is sufficient, and I trust that You can truly wash me clean. I return to You now, and choose to follow You, fully.

I will not hide in shame but instead stay close to You and invite your Holy Spirit to continue revealing truth into my heart and mind. Jesus, I acknowledge You are the way, the truth, and the life. Please lead me on this journey of discovery and transformation from the inside out. Thank You for promising to finish the work You started in me. Amen."

Truth Darts

- **GOD DIDN'T AUTHOR THE LIES I BELIEVE.**

  "Behold, You desire truth in the innermost being, and in secret You will make wisdom known to me." (Psalm 51:6)

- **THE FATHER DESIRES MY FREEDOM!**

  "It was for freedom that Christ set us free; therefore keep standing firm and do not be subject again to a yoke of slavery." (Galatians 5:1)

- **I AM REDEEMED. THERE IS NO SHAME OR CONDEMNATION BECAUSE I AM IN CHRIST.**

  "Therefore there is now no condemnation at all for those who are in Christ Jesus. For the law of the Spirit of life in Christ Jesus has set you free from the law of sin and of death." (Romans 8:1-2)

- **HE MADE A WAY FOR ME TO LIVE IN VICTORY!**

  "Therefore if anyone is in Christ, this person is a new creation; the old things passed away; behold, new things have come." (2 Corinthians 5:17)

- **I WILL TRUST THE FATHER AND FOLLOW THE HOLY SPIRIT'S LEADING.**

  "Work out your own salvation with fear and trembling; for it is God who is at work in you, both to desire and to work for His good pleasure." (Philippians 2:12-13)

CHAPTER 4

JUST LIKE JESUS... WHO, ME?

"Being like Jesus seems unrealistic and unattainable. God can't possibly expect me to be like Jesus here and now."

Recently, God led me to update my wardrobe. "Think of it as an upgrade," He encouraged me. My birthday was coming up, and my mom was going to treat me to a shopping day out. Immediately, I knew God wanted to teach me something important: In order to make space for new things, I had to first sort through the old. So, on a rainy Saturday morning, I ventured into my closet with a big garbage bag and some determination.

Sorting was tedious. There were many "okay" but not "great" pieces. Some items worked in past seasons but didn't fit anymore or had become outdated. Others were comfortable but not quite my style anymore. "What will I wear this with?" and "How will I accessorize the outfit?" I asked my daughter, who stepped in to help. I carefully considered each piece, and she eagerly encouraged me to let many things go. Releasing them was challenging but also exciting, especially when I imagined the upcoming shopping day and the new clothes that would better suit me!

The Lie Explained

Beliefs are like clothing items that hang in our closets. Some Christians don't even know what has taken up mental space until they begin sorting it all out. Their identity beliefs are a mix of ideas collected over the years. And just like a wardrobe badly in need of an upgrade, their beliefs of themselves in Christ might need some special attention, too! In truth, God wants more for His children than "comfortable" and just "good enough." He wants all of us clothed in His best, though many don't understand what that really means.

Some Christians believe Jesus was a great teacher who lived long ago—He was. They think He taught people how to live good lives—He did. And they likely trust Him as their Savior—that He is! Yet, He is so much more. Because they don't fully comprehend their own identity as God's beloved child, they may not connect with the biblical accounts of Jesus's life. They don't realize they can encounter Him intimately or experience a real relationship with Him. They aren't sure they're called to live like Him, or do the things He did.

Though they're briefly curious if there's more of God for here and now, they squelch the questions. They are comfortable and don't pursue growth with Jesus. They neglect nurturing His Holy Spirit's work in them. And then they wonder where their passion for God and others has gone. They settle for the belief that abundant life with Jesus is for another day, or for sometime in the future. *Why should I change now, when I could wait for Heaven?* They ask. But instead of being transformed into the image of Christ, they have conformed Him into theirs.

This is how it happened for me, anyway. I was comfortable doing good works for God but didn't realize there was more of Him to know here and now. Until I put in the effort to uncover the lies and become like Him. *How can life be fruitful and yet so simple?* I wondered. *Won't following Jesus either be awkward or require a life of being "in ministry?"* Before I understood the abundant life Jesus intends for all of us, I even thought supernaturally inspired Christians seemed a little strange. Like my closet needed an update, sometimes our beliefs about who we are in Christ are worn out. And it could be time for an identity upgrade.

Truth from God's Word

Understanding the Way of Jesus is what abundant life is all about. Many Christians are busy being busy, and missing the main point. While reading the Bible, going to church, singing worship songs, and serving God are all valuable aspects of growing in relationship with Him, they aren't the primary purpose of our Christian life. None of us are created to just go through the motions with God. Honestly, it's exactly the opposite. Regular people like you and me are meant to realize the same powerful, fulfilling, and fruitful lives with God in the same way Jesus did. In fact, experiencing Christlikeness in everyday life is our God-given birthright as His children.

From the beginning of time, God had a plan and revealed it to us in His Word. His purpose for humanity is evidenced throughout scripture. The first man and woman were created in His image, formed by His own hands, and breathed into by His very breath. (Genesis 1:26-27 and 2:7) They walked with God and talked with Him. And they encountered Him intimately, face-to-face. "God blessed them; and God said to them, 'Be fruitful and multiply, and fill the earth, and subdue it; and rule over the fish of the sea and over the birds of the sky and over every living thing that moves on the earth.' " (Genesis 1:28)

Unlike every other living creature, the first humans were set apart to share in God's likeness and entrusted with the care of the Earth. God blessed them. And He gave them an assignment to accomplish with Him. They were to be fruitful, to multiply, to fill the Earth, and to govern it, as they were provided for. Everything they needed to succeed was taken into account, including the most perfect environment for them to live and thrive in. They were God's beloved image-bearers on the Earth.

God spoke with Noah and walked with him and talked with him. Later, God called Abram out from his own people to the land He chose. Abram walked with God, and they made a covenant. God promised that all the nations of the earth would be blessed through him. (Genesis 17) Later in the book of Exodus, we read how Moses also encountered God: "So the Lord used to speak to Moses face-to-face, just as a man speaks to his friend." (Exodus 33:11) And through their relationship, God's Law was introduced, which eventually revealed our need for Jesus. Throughout scripture, we see many heroes of the faith who walked with God and talked with Him.

Just like them, we are created in God's image and are meant to walk with Him and talk with Him, and to intimately encounter Him everyday. And we have been assigned the same mandate: To be fruitful and multiply, to fill the Earth and to govern it. But what about now? How can we know the way? Jesus is our standard; and though we messed up, He offers grace. When Jesus died, He took on our flesh nature, and we died with Him. (Romans 6:4-7) Then, when He was resurrected, we were also raised and seated with Him "in the heavenly places in Christ Jesus." (Ephesians 2:6) Truly, we've been liberated and are set free to live by His Spirit! (Galatians 5:18, 25) Through Him, we can know fellowship with the Father, just as Jesus did! It is imperative that the revelation of this truth becomes clear, for it is the crux, the hinge point, the deciding factor, for apprehending the abundant life that is available for all of us.

Consequences for Disregarding the Truth

Taking a good look, we'll notice just how misunderstanding our identity as His beloved children has caused serious consequences. Generally, believers have settled. At best, they've spent their time doing things that seem important but aren't actually producing fullness, the very fruit of Jesus. Or, because they've measured success by human efforts, they strive for power and positions and then feel condemned when they seem to fail. *I can never be like Jesus, anyway,* they think. *After all, He was a perfect human, and I am not.* And by this, some Christians have become lazily lukewarm and sabotaged a lifestyle of real faith.

These consequences have had a detrimental effect on the corporate body of Christ, too—for centuries. Believers haven't been faithful image-bearers. Generally, we haven't been formed into His likeness and have sorely misrepresented Him. In some cases we've highlighted our favorite scriptures, used His words as weapons against each other, even using His Name to accomplish our own foolish human agendas. We haven't practiced what Jesus preached and have been distracted away from growing up into Him—who is the Head over the church—and from attaining the true unity of faith. (Ephesians 4:13-16)

Without faith, it's impossible to please God.

(Hebrews 11:6) In fact, none of us can measure up to the life of Jesus without Him. We are instructed to take off "the old self" and actually "put on the Lord Jesus Christ." (Ephesians 4:22, Romans 13:14) Truthfully, our human efforts will never be enough to make us more like Jesus. For Jesus alone is the physical manifestation of God's nature, the very expression of who our Father is. Only Jesus can be like Jesus, truly. Only He can transform us into His very image. As we live according to His Spirit, we will realize His powerful, fulfilling, and fruitful life. Talk about a wardrobe upgrade!

The Holy Characteristics of Jesus Revealed

Understanding my need for Him led me to ask the Holy Spirit to reveal Jesus to me personally. Though I had known about Jesus my whole life, it required some deep digging. "Since I can only be like You as I know You, please show me who You really are." He responded by highlighting His holy characteristics to meditate on.

First, Jesus knew He was His Father's Son, and He never lost sight of His identity. This empowered his faithfulness. Even when He faced trials, He knew how to overcome. For "man does not live on bread alone but on every word that comes from the mouth of the Lord." (Deuteronomy 8:3) In the same way, pursuing a relationship with the Father means never losing sight of who we are in Him. Like Jesus, He calls us His beloved children. And believing anything less than this about ourselves is a lie. "For all who are being led by the Spirit of God, these are sons and daughters of God. For you have not received a spirit of slavery leading to fear again, but you have received a spirit of adoption as sons and daughters by which we cry out, 'Abba! Father!' The Spirit Himself testifies with our spirit that we are children of God." (Romans 8:14-16) We must become enraptured by His love and never lose sight of our true identity in Christ. Just like Jesus fed on every word of the Father, so we must take in the life of Jesus and sustain ourselves by truth.

Second, He highlighted how Jesus encountered the Father face-to-face. Not only did He know God, He knew Him *intimately*. Jesus often stole away to be alone with the Father in quiet places. Jesus relied on and lived by the very words of God. Just like Him, so we also must discipline ourselves to know the Father by being alone with Him in stillness, to learn to know Him and His Word. When I was a teenager, a friend encouraged our youth group to practice spending fifteen minutes each morning in the quiet, just listening for God and learning to know His voice. This habit I've adopted has helped me experience God more intimately. At times, beholding Him this way has required extreme vulnerability from me, as He has invited me to let go of my own expectations, "Dear daughter, release your judgments to me. And I will replace your stony heart with mine." Just as gold is refined by fire, my heart becomes new as I allow His holy love to burn away in me all that isn't from Him. Encountering Him has required patience from me, as I learn to wait on Him and rest in His presence.

And third, Jesus never underestimated His authority, because He knew its intended purpose. When He unrolled the scroll in the temple and read from Isaiah 61, He didn't stumble over His words. To the contrary, understanding who He was—His Father's Son—empowered Jesus to boldly proclaim the truth about Himself. He announced, "The Spirit of the Lord God is upon me, because the Lord anointed me." (Isaiah 61:1) And, just like Jesus, we are also heirs of God. Through Him, we have access to all the same rights and privileges our Father gave Him. "The Spirit Himself testifies with our spirit that we are children of God, and if children, heirs also, heirs of God and fellow heirs with Christ." (Romans 8:17) We must have faith. What was spoken of Jesus is true for us, too. Confidence is not pride. Rather, knowing who we are means we're strong in Him! We cannot allow false humility to hinder us from being bold and loving in our surrendered service.

Do you know that our Father created each one of us to be His beloved children and to know Him—to know Him intimately? You can approach Him face-to-face, breathe deeply, and hold His gaze. As you allow Him to look into your soul, receive His loving words. Remain in Him, and He will surely remain in you. (John 15:4) And just like Jesus, you will also be empowered to declare that *"the Spirit of the Lord is upon me, because He has anointed me to bring good news to the poor. He has sent me to proclaim release to captives, and recovery of sight to the blind, to set free those who are oppressed, to proclaim the favorable year of the Lord."* (Luke 4:18-19)

Intimate Encounters

COMMUNION

"Dear Child, I know you have tried to walk out your Christian life so faithfully. And, from outward appearances, you have done it well. My precious one, Jesus alone is the standard for abundant life, and He already accomplished the only necessary work. You are forever covered by the righteousness of Jesus, and there is nothing more for you to do. So, you may let go of the pressure to perform. Simply rest in relationship with Me. I do have plans and purposes for your life, but that isn't why I love you. I love you simply because you are my child. Your only need is to surrender and keep in step with the Holy Spirit. And as you do, your life will flow in the same anointing of Jesus. You will carry great authority to do as He did, as you live and move and set your being in Him."

PRAYER FOR HEALING

"Father God, I am humbled. I trust that the very life of Jesus is God's only standard for abundant life, and He made the way for me. Your robe of righteousness is enough for me. I repent for living in mediocrity. I will rise and walk away from the lies that have kept me bound to earthly thinking. Your life provides the fullness, and I will remain in a closely connected relationship with Your Holy Spirit. I want my life to have an impact on future generations, so I will run my race with a holy desire to be fully healed, to live whole and set free from the inside out. As Your child, I am a blessed carrier of Your heavenly glory on Earth. Amen."

Truth Darts

- **JESUS IS THE STANDARD FOR ABUNDANT LIFE.**

"The thief comes only to steal and kill and destroy; I came so that they would have life, and have it abundantly." (John 10:10)

- **THERE IS NO REAL LIFE OUTSIDE OF LIVING IN RELATIONSHIP WITH MY HEAVENLY FATHER.**

"Jesus said to him, 'I am the way, and the truth, and the life; no one comes to the Father except through Me. If you had known Me, you would have known My Father also; from now on you know Him, and have seen Him.' " (John 14:6-7)

- **HE COVERED ME WITH HIS OWN RIGHTEOUSNESS.**

"He made Him who knew no sin to be sin in our behalf, so that we might become the righteousness of God in Him." (2 Corinthians 5:21)
"I will rejoice greatly in the Lord, my soul will be joyful in my God; for He has clothed me with garments of salvation, He has wrapped me with a robe of righteousness." (Isaiah 61:10)

- **MY FULLY SURRENDERED LIFE IS MY GRATEFUL RESPONSE FOR HIS SACRIFICE.**

"Therefore, I urge you, brothers and sisters, in view of God's mercy, to offer your bodies as a living sacrifice, holy and pleasing to God—this is your true and proper worship. Do not conform to the pattern of this world, but be transformed by the renewing of your mind. Then you will be able to test and

approve what God's will is—his good, pleasing and perfect will." (Romans 12:1-2)

- **MY BEST IS ALLOWING HIM TO LIVE HIS LIFE FULLY FREE IN ME AND THROUGH ME.**

"I have been crucified with Christ; and it is no longer I who live, but Christ lives in me; and the life which I now live in the flesh I live by faith in the Son of God, who loved me and gave Himself up for me." (Galatians 2:20)

CHAPTER 5

CUTTING TIES

"I don't need to cut ties with my
painful past or work at releasing
unforgiveness to receive inner healing."

Once, our Thai team gathered expectantly in an upper room at the Juniper Tree in Chiang Mai. A friend from the United States had come to visit for our annual retreat. During prayer, he saw something like a vision of a blue songbird. The bird sang sweetly and attempted to fly. But each time she ascended, invisible strings held her tight and consistently pulled her back towards the ground. Though she appeared to be flying, she couldn't actually take flight—she wasn't free to soar. Attempting to break free, she furiously flapped and fluttered her wings; but the harder she tried, the more tired and entangled she became. Our friend's words continued while his voice trailed off—for me—and I heard the Father speaking... "My child, you are like that songbird. Deep emotional trauma has crippled you from becoming truly free as you're meant to be. While you appear to be flying, soul wounds from your past have held you back, and they must be severed so you can soar with Me."

The Lie Explained

To a degree, many believers are like that songbird. Inner heart wounds have tied them tight and bound them to their pain. They are still bombarded by hurtful words or painful rejection from their past. Or they bristle at the names of those who hurt them or took advantage of their innocence. They desperately attempt to release the traumatic memories. Perhaps they read self-help books and listen to podcasts—none of which has helped. Even after all their effort, they're still stuck on the same old lines. Though they say the right words and try to release the unforgiveness, they aren't certain how to really let go. Their emotions feel severely damaged. And even though they know how they *should* respond, they feel powerless to break free from past trauma.

It's true that "trauma" has become a common buzzword in our culture, and we should not settle into victim mentality, blaming our past for our current struggles. But, it is also true that many times believers unnecessarily accept residual effects of trauma wounds and allow consequences to hinder them from experiencing real freedom in Christ. Although abundant life is available as soon as we receive Him, true abundant life with Jesus comes through the intentional pursuit of personal inner healing and wholeness—which is often a gradual process.

Christians, especially, know that God is our healer. And like I was taught, maybe they know how to pray for God to heal headaches and sniffles. But what many don't realize is that God also wants to heal our heart wounds! Others may not understand how to remain in communion with the Holy Spirit throughout the often difficult process of receiving their emotional healing. Although a sincere prayer of faith was whispered during worship, many don't continue to believe and pray, and pray and believe. They give up when the pain doesn't disappear right away. And instead of participating with God for their inner healing, they allow distance in their relationship with God, further accentuating the nagging pains from their past.

Deferred hope has led many believers into despair, and has even caused some to be skeptical towards God. They doubt His love for them and wonder if He really is as good as they thought. Perhaps they laugh their pain away, allowing sarcasm to mask their emotional insecurity. Or they numb the pain and treat their symptoms, all while settling into unbelief. It's true, when there are unresolved wounds, looking back hurts. But, burying the pain deeper only allows the past to continue—causing more damage and passing it on to others.

Truth from God's Word

God loves His children and wants people everywhere to experience His abundant life. What many Christians don't yet fully grasp, though, is the degree our Father intends for each part of our lives to be affected by His grace. Not only does God desire that every person prospers spiritually, but also that we are made whole mentally, emotionally, relationally—and in all the other ways, too! Encountering Christ fully affects every area of our lives. And abundant life is intended to prosper us from the inside out, even as our souls prosper. (1 John 3:2, 3 John 1:2)

Throughout scripture, the Father reveals how deeply He cares for us. Just as Israel was God's chosen covenant people through whom He first communicated His character and displayed His great power, so also are we now grafted into His covenant. Through Christ, all of us have become "a chosen people, a royal priesthood, a holy nation, a people for God's own possession." (1 Peter 2:9) The scriptures meant for God's chosen people are also for us—as we are chosen. Our Father loves us with an everlasting love that cares deeply about all aspects of our lives. (Jeremiah 31:3) When we hurt, He hurts, and He longs to gather us, "just as a hen *gathers* her young under her wings." (Luke 13:34) When we feel pain and turmoil, He understands and longs to hold us and heal us. He promises to bind up bruises, release the captives, free the prisoners, and restore our very health. (Isaiah 30:26, Isaiah 61:1, Jeremiah

30:7) For, "He heals the brokenhearted and binds up their wounds." (Psalm 147:3)

Because humans are complex beings, the intricate aspects of our psyche are all interconnected. Science has proven that even our bodies hold onto unaddressed pain from the past. Even when face-to-face encounters with the Spirit of Truth are uncomfortable, each of us must undergo deep emotional surgery to experience the full freedom Jesus made available. Wholeness requires diligence, and finding broken or missing pieces requires perseverance. Therefore, it's imperative to intentionally and proactively pursue inner healing.

Consequences for Disregarding the Truth

It is possible to know God's love but miss out on apprehending the complete, abundant life Jesus promised because we are unwilling to cut ties with the habits and belief systems we inherited through our heart wounds. Unless we intentionally seek healing for the places where the effects of sin still fester, the lies which cloud our vision of who God is and who we are in Him will hinder us from experiencing the full abundant life He created us for. Inner healing is a continual growth process, so being hasty or concerned with how we appear—while God is working—does not produce the results of our wholeness. We must surrender, even in our brokenness. Just like dross is extracted when gold is refined in the fire, we must remain intentionally present in Christ while

God carefully extracts impurities and we can trust His presence to hold us steady through the holy, purifying process. There's no need to rush Him, for His work inside us is deeply more valuable than anything He desires to do through us. The wholeness—and holiness—of our own soul is what He's after.

Often, we're quick to dismiss the seemingly small effects of past residue as personality quirks, the result of us being ourselves. *It's just the way I am. God must have made me this way.* But real freedom comes by deliberately allowing the light of God to shine in every place and agreeing with His truth. We can't give God some parts of our heart and not others. In truth, compartmentalizing our consecration to the Father inhibits the work He desires to bring forth to completion within us. It is His good pleasure to work within us. He is not giving up, so we can't either! (Philippians 2:13, Philippians 1:6)

Participation in the Healing Process

Trauma comes in all shapes and sizes. In the same way a broken arm requires proper assessment before the cast can be set for healing, so it is with inner healing. Soul wounds require purposeful evaluation, an invitation for the Holy Spirit to come in and assess our situations; and ultimately, active participation with Him in the healing process, so that wholeness can come forth.

Sometimes, trauma goes undetected and remains in subconscious memories until the

Father reveals them. First, learning to listen and pay close attention to *our* inner voice is valuable for making purposeful evaluations. *What is going on inside of me? What clues are my feelings suggesting in this situation?* In truth, feelings are godly gifts that can indicate areas in need of healing. They help us understand what's going on inside our psyche and uncover the lies that hinder our health and happiness. While emotions aren't necessarily true, it's valuable to first validate their reality so we can test them against God's Word. Too often, Christians especially, have developed mistrust of their own feelings. Like I did, they could have been taught to ignore or stuff them. But by undervaluing ourselves as emotional beings, we've disregarded God's design for humanness. And we've created cultures that idolize stoicism and guardedness in our interactions with God and each other.

We can determinedly believe our heavenly Father cares, and place our full trust in Him. He knows we are human, and He is patient and kind. He doesn't belittle us in our weakness or push us away when we fail. In fact, most of the book of Psalms is the recorded journal of David, the very one called "a man after God's own heart." (1 Samuel 13:14) There, we notice that David wasn't afraid of his feelings. Rather, he knew God was his safe place, and he trusted Him. He welcomed God into the deepest parts of his heart and passionately poured out his complaint. (Psalm 142) David wasn't scolded for his vulnerable approach with our Father, and neither are we. Just like him, we don't have to fear feeling deep emotion. We can trust God as our safe place; He knows us, and He cares. We can passionately express our trauma wounds with our Father, too. As we do, His Holy Spirit helps us evaluate where false belief systems have settled.

Second, purposeful invitation of the Holy Spirit into our healing is the key for learning where we're still stuck. As our hearts soften and open to Him, our Father reveals the wounds and connected lies, like invisible strings that have tightly tied us down. And, when He does, we must partner with Him in cutting those ties—agreement with Him is crucial for apprehending the abundant life He designed us for. We can trust God and pray as David did, "Search me, God, and know my heart; put me to the test and know my anxious thoughts; and see if there is any hurtful way in me, and lead me in the everlasting way." (Psalm 139:23-24)

Third, healing requires a full pursuit of Jesus with the tools He provides. And, intentionally participating with Him in cutting ties and pursuing freedom will always produce good fruit. Psalm 23, a well-known scripture passage, briefly summarizes how David faithfully participated with God throughout his life. He knew God guided him, and he also trusted that God's presence followed him. Apprehending that he was surrounded by God's goodness, he declared, "The Lord is my shepherd, I will not be in need. He lets me lie down in green pastures; He leads me beside quiet waters. He restores my soul; He guides me in the paths of righteousness for the sake of His name. Even though I walk through the valley of the shadow of death, I fear no evil, for You are with me; Your rod and Your staff, they comfort me. You prepare a table before me in the presence of my enemies; You have anointed my head with oil; My cup overflows. Certainly goodness and faithfulness will follow me all the days of my life, and my dwelling will be in the house of the Lord forever." (Psalm 23)

Tools for Growth

There is no set formula for becoming emotionally free. But I briefly share these tools, so that you may be inspired to find what works for you. As God gently worked inside me, He revealed where insecurity from painful childhood memories was hiding. Honestly, it was frustrating. At points I asked God, *"Why did you make me this way? It hurts to feel so deeply."* I became uncomfortable. I realized that it was no longer okay to play the victim or shift blame when I felt hurt or alone. Since my freedom was dependent on facing it head-on, I accepted the painful emotions and took personal responsibility for what I allowed to settle into my heart and mind. God was my Shield and Defender.

Remaining in Him throughout the healing process was crucial, and so I also remembered the spiritual disciplines I had learned, practicing them as a means for recognizing God's near presence even through suffering. I realized the disciplines were not obligatory tasks to check off my to-do list, but tools for encountering His Truth. Here are a few key ones that helped me retrain my heart and mind. I encourage you to consider making these disciplines a priority in your journey, too.

— Journaling

Like David, I wrote out my thoughts and feelings with transparency, which helped me connect with my soul. As I journaled, the places inside that weren't in alignment with God's truth became more apparent. And though it sometimes stung to see it on paper, at least I had a clear direction: to amend and reform the places in my heart that still needed to come under His lordship. Often, tears streamed down onto the pages as I recorded deep thoughts and emotions. *I trust You, God. Even though this hurts so much, I know that You are good and faithful. I will say "Yes" to following Your way, even in entering my very own* "valley of the shadow of death." (Psalm 23:4)

— Fasting and Prayer

Practiced together, fasting and prayer have been powerful tools to quiet the voice of my flesh. Emptying myself of prideful ego has initiated greater spiritual hunger and created a heart posture that was more receptive towards God. Interestingly, as I have practiced fasting and prayer, I've noticed that my flesh usually cries out for whatever I depended on apart from Him. And the Holy Spirit used that process to re-awaken me to my subconscious inner life and will. *Father, I only hunger for You and Your ways. I want to walk through this painful process in the very way Jesus did. I cling to You. Sustain me, I pray.* And as I encountered Him there, He patiently revealed the unhealthy patterns, and He sustained me through the process of retraining my heart and mind after His truth.

— *Spiritual Warfare*

At times, spiritual warfare was necessary for tearing down demonic strongholds that were built in my mind through prolonged partnership with the enemy. And so I spoke out loud, "I have agreed with the enemy's lie_____, though now I recognize my position in Christ–seated 'far above all rule and authority and power and dominion.' (Ephesians 1:21) And therefore, I take a stand in my rightful authority as a daughter of God and push the enemy out of my mind by the power and blood of Jesus Christ." Not only was it important to remove the demonic influence but also to root out the lies that permitted the enemy to oppress me in the first place. Because spiritual battles are strenuous, it was extremely valuable to invite godly friends to stand with me.

— *Worship*

True worship is powerful. Ultimately, it is about setting our hearts on God. And yet, lifting His Name also brings forth healing and life within us.

Focusing on Him nourishes our soul, because our hearts and minds are lifted when we intentionally encounter Him. For me, often when I least feel like worshipping God is when I most need to. Choosing to honor God above my own situation is an act of surrender, a holy sacrifice. Even when I don't feel like it, I worship. For He alone is worthy. I've found that as He is crowned "Lord over all," (Romans 10:12) the significance of my own circumstances fades in comparison.

— *Meditating on Scripture*

Sometimes worship can also take a restful posture. For me, scripture set to music immerses me in the peaceful atmosphere of Heaven. "Soaking," as it has been called, has refreshed my soul so many times. Especially when we lived overseas, I took regular personal retreats to a nearby hotel room—not nearly as expensive as in the U.S. These special moments with God were beautiful times of quiet sabbath rest. *I'm listening for You, God. Turn my heart to hear Your gentle whisperings. Speak to me as I rest in You.* And then I waited. Typically, I read scripture or simply lay on the bed, meditating on God's truth set to music. I often fell into a deep and peaceful sleep as God restored my soul. This is a wonderful discipline to practice before falling asleep each night, too.

— *Memorizing Scripture*

Scripture is a powerful tool for tearing down strongholds. (2 Corinthians 10:3-5) As a teenager, I was introduced to some of Dr. Neil T. Anderson's books. Often, I encountered God as I stood face-to-face with Him in front of my bedroom mirror. The Holy Spirit came near and remained present with me as I repeated the truth of His words into my own spirit, sometimes for long periods until I finally believed it. As I applied God's truth to false thought patterns, the Holy Spirit has miraculously transformed my mind. He rewrote my worn-out beliefs and created new pathways in me according to His Word. By memorizing scriptures, I've gained a useful and reliable weapon against the enemy. Even now, wielding God's Word as a double-edged sword is my best defense against the temptation of old triggers. (Hebrews 4:12)

Just as Jesus was sustained as He practiced knowing God's presence throughout His everyday moments, so can we. These tools can lead Christians to encounter the Father intimately, and more consistently. In truth, they are the very weapons to combat the lies of the enemy. The truth is, God's grace is sufficient, even for overcoming past trauma wounds. And facing our fears *with* Him while allowing Him to be our Shield and Defender strengthens us. Just like the beautiful, blue songbird, each of us are meant to soar! For the glory of the One and Only, may it be so.

Intimate Encounters

COMMUNION

"Dear Child, I know you have experienced pain, and many of the wounds have been buried deep inside. Though you did not see Me then, I was right there with you the whole time. And I want your freedom. By taking time to evaluate your feelings connected to trauma, you will learn what you've stuffed down and how it is negatively affecting your life. Will you allow Me to be the searchlight to show you all that's there, exposing the lies to reveal My truth? Can you entrust every part of your heart—the good, the bad, and even the ugly—to Me? Though cutting ties with the pain of your past wounds may hurt temporarily, it will bring forth so much healing. Truly, I work all things together for good. O, I have such hope for you, my precious one."

PRAYER FOR HEALING

"God, You are a good Father who loves me. I haven't always known this, but now I do. And, Your love is so much more than I can comprehend. As I evaluate all that is happening in the innermost places of my being, I will not do it independently. I will dig deep and, no matter what it looks like, allow You to expose the painful trauma from my past, so You can heal me by Your truth. Though You may lead me through seemingly difficult and possibly painful circumstances, I trust that You are revealing where my heart is, because You desire my freedom and growth.

Help me. I know now that the work You want to do in me matters more than the work You will do through me, and so I surrender my need to understand or be in charge.

Like the Psalmist, 'I invite your searching gaze into my heart. Examine me through and through; find out everything that may be hidden within me. Put me to the test and sift through all my anxious cares. See if there is any path of pain I'm walking on, and lead me back to your glorious, everlasting way—the path that brings me back to you.' (Psalm 139:23-24 TPT) Amen."

Truth Darts

- **EVALUATING FEELINGS CONNECTED TO TRAUMA IS A CRUCIAL PART OF THE HEALING PROCESS.**

"Search me, God, and know my heart; Put me to the test and know my anxious thoughts; And see if there is any hurtful way in me, And lead me in the everlasting way." (Psalm 139:23-24)

- **GOD IS A GOOD FATHER AND CAN BE TRUSTED WITH MY HEART.**

"As far as the east is from the west, so far has He removed our wrongdoings from us. Just as a father has compassion on his children, so the Lord has compassion on those who fear Him." (Psalm 103:12-13)

- **I WILL PARTNER WITH HIM TO UNCOVER MY TRUE IDENTITY.**

"Lord, You have searched me and known me. You know when I sit down and when I get up; You understand my thoughts from far away. You scrutinize my path and my lying down, And are acquainted with all my ways. Even before there is a word on my tongue, Behold, Lord, You know it all. You have encircled me behind and in front, And placed Your hand upon me. Such knowledge is too wonderful for me; It is too high, I cannot comprehend it. Where can I go from Your Spirit?" (Psalm 139:1-7)

- **CUTTING TIES WITH THE PAST MIGHT BE PAINFUL BUT WORTH IT.**

"Consider it all joy, my brothers and sisters, when you encounter various trials, knowing that the testing of your faith produces endurance. And let endurance have its perfect result, so that you may be perfect and complete, lacking in nothing." (James 1:2-4)

- **KNOWING THE TRUTH BRINGS REAL FREEDOM.**

"And you will know the truth, and the truth will set you free." (John 8:32)

CHAPTER 6

BEING A GOOD GIRL

"I am loved based on my own good deeds."

One particular morning in Thailand, I sat in the quiet stillness with my steaming cup of coffee and peered outside. Amidst the hazy heat of a Thai sunrise, monks weaved their way from the local temple onto the waking streets. Slowly, they trailed along, collecting food for the day from commoners, who scooped up spoons full of rice for them. By giving food to the monks, and by lighting incense to appease the ancestor spirits, Thai Buddhists "make merit." For them, goodness is earned. They live in the hope that their good and bad deeds eventually balance out and cancel into nothingness—nirvana.

As I sat and pondered the scene through my window, the realization came to me: *I am tired. As a wife and mother in this faraway place, being a good Christian feels especially difficult. Finding enough time to pray and read my Bible is challenging. And I don't get out to "do ministry" with the others as often as I want to, either. Am I doing enough for Him?* I wondered.

I loved Jesus. And obedience had led me to follow Him to the other side of the world, and to serve Him faithfully. Though on a smaller scale, my inner spiritual world was strikingly similar to those of my Thai neighbors. Like them, I was striving by my efforts to be good enough, to balance out my bad deeds. Sometimes, it felt like I was "making merit" and appeasing God to gain His acceptance—and sadly, earn His favor.

The Lie Explained

While you may not live in Buddhist culture, you've likely watched others attempt to make merit with God. They trust Him for salvation but their rightness with Him is still based on their own goodness. They try to earn His favor by their many works. Many Christians quote the scriptures and trust that grace is "not a result of works, so that no one may boast," (Ephesians 2:9) yet they judge themselves and others based on efforts and good deeds. While they say actions can't make God love His children more than He already does, they still strive.

Every year at church camp, I knelt at the front altar and hoped and prayed I could be good enough for God. When I did good things like memorize scripture, go to church every Sunday, or read my daily "devotions," I felt like God was pleased. Like He was more proud of me, somehow. But when I failed Him or fell into sin, I thought He was disappointed or withholding His love. And I was sent spiraling down into a pit of despair until I could prove my repentance, hoping my own good works would balance out the guilt. Rather than trust that my identity was solid in Christ, my emotions became the barometer. Life according to this orientation felt like riding a spiritual rollercoaster.

In the same way that bringing my Bible and being a witness for Jesus earned me star stickers in Sunday School, many Christians have chosen a life of service for its rewards. Feeling like God is pleased by their good deeds makes them feel safe and secure, and so performing for Him has become their way of life. Their life with God has been organized into an obligatory checklist, rather than celebrated as an exciting faith-filled adventure. And their joy is gone.

Truth from God's Word

In the previous chapter, we learned the necessity of putting forth effort to cut ties with wounds from our past so we can experience personal breakthroughs. But, investing ourselves to overcome trauma is very different from striving for God's love and acceptance. Let's not confuse these realities. In fact, grace to pursue inner healing comes by first understanding true identity in Christ.

The truth is, nothing anyone can ever do

could dampen or deter the Father's deep love. He is pleased simply because we are His children. Not only does rightness with Him come through Jesus but so also peace and harmony and intimacy. In the beginning, God created mankind and pronounced them "very good," and there was harmony in relationship with Him. (Genesis 1:31) Then fear, separation, and disharmony entered by sin; and only His perfection can heal this breach. But in fact, Jesus's sinless sacrifice *proved* His love and revealed our worth. He perfectly covered our sins. Though we can not earn salvation, we must know we have been deemed worthy of it by proof of God's own grace gift—His own Son's life—on our behalf. Through Him we are saved and redeemed forever! (1 Peter 1:18, 19)

"For what the Law could not do, weak as it was through the flesh, God did: sending His own Son in the likeness of sinful flesh and as an offering for sin, He condemned sin in the flesh, so that the requirement of the Law might be fulfilled in us who do not walk according to the flesh but according to the Spirit." (Romans 8:3-4)

Consequences for Disregarding the Truth

Misunderstanding what grace is has caused serious spiritual and real-life ramifications. Though many Christians mentally assent to receiving God's salvation by grace through faith, sometimes their actions reveal an interpretation of grace which is more akin to appeasement. We'll explore this soon.

Since grace is the fundamental factor for our faith in Jesus, careful distinctions must be made here. So, what is grace? According to Merriam-Webster, grace is defined thus: "Unmerited divine assistance given to humans for their regeneration or sanctification: a virtue coming from God: a state of sanctification enjoyed through divine assistance."

Another well-known interpretation of grace, though, is that: *"Grace is the unmerited favor of God,"* which comes by way of the "doctrines of grace" from a Reformed theological tradition.[1]

While it's true that grace can not be earned, some mistakenly interpret people as being unworthy of God's grace. And the general understanding is that God requires the punishment of sin on our behalf, before our Father can love us. No matter how sincere Christians are, some believe mankind is naturally sinful, and may even believe people are loveable first—and only through—the substitutionary atonement of Jesus.[2] I know I did; I thought God could only look upon me, a sinner, through the lens of Jesus. But grace interpreted this way appears more like fear-based appeasement. Now let's look at a definition of appeasement.

According to Merriam-Webster, appeasement means "to pacify, conciliate – especially : to make concessions – to someone (such as an aggressor or

---

1   https://learn.ligonier.org/articles/what-grace
2   Although deep, theological discussion is not the point of this work, understanding where foundational beliefs stem from can be helpful for finding freedom from lies.

a critic) often at the sacrifice of principles." Often, this word connotes a superior being requiring something from another—typically an inferior—who is obligated to satisfy the requirements of the superior before they can be considered worthy.

How is this important to our conversation? Because for centuries, Christians have viewed grace through a smudged lens, and our perspectives of God and ourselves have been shaped accordingly. Some Christians feel shameful. They believe they're unworthy to be loved, although our loving Father proved we are. And they feel less valuable to Him than His actions suggest! These false perceptions have bound many Christians to fear rather than lifting them from it. Separation beliefs have created distance from God and each other, though He calls us near. And generally, we've relegated ourselves to the realm of "sinners saved by grace," rather than celebrating our freedom as the very "Sons and Daughters of God that we are!" (Galatians 3:26)

In fact, some deep-seated religious doctrines may not truly represent our Father. And these ungodly worldviews have predisposed many to believe the lies they do.[3]

---

3   I have only touched on the concept of original sin and Jesus's substitutionary atonement. And although a deeper study could prove beneficial, that is not our purpose here. For more on this topic, please refer to the book Precious in His Sight: A Fresh Look at the Nature of Humanity by Harold Eberle.

Personal Beliefs Aligned
With God's Heart

And what is our remedy? I propose that Christians must willingly allow our core beliefs to be challenged. Before we can fully apprehend our freedom, we must ponder the questions. *If humanity is so undeserving of God's love, then why has He noticeably and intimately pursued relationship with us? Doesn't His pursuit of us imply we are extremely valuable to Him?*

Therefore, as we evaluate the concept of grace, and as we allow God's Holy Spirit to speak truth about who He is and who we are, it would be helpful to adjust our understanding and therefore reestablish a more accurate working definition of grace—such as: "*God supernaturally empowering us to do what we cannot do in our own strength.*" (Steve Burris – pastor, spiritual leader, and friend)

Since intimacy with God as our loving Father has not been readily accepted by many Christians, believers must seek to know Him anew. And to realize His grace for encountering Him and allowing Him to uncover the—often subtle—motivations of our hearts; and then choosing truthful awareness over falsehood. As we do, He'll reveal the counterfeit crutches, the ways we've justified ourselves and attempted to produce our own rightness apart from Him.

Truly, God requires nothing more than our simple surrender to the grace He has provided. None of our efforts could ever produce the real and lasting fruit that comes by simply abiding in Him. And so, we can let go and simply lean into Jesus, and enjoy the process of relationship with Him! Just as Jesus knew the secret of remaining in the Father, He welcomes each of us into the very same close connection He and the Father share—into face-to-face truth encounters with Him.

Corporate Beliefs Aligned With God's Heart

Similar to our Thai friends plagued by their bondage of appeasing ancestor spirits and "making merit," the modern Christian Church has become distracted. And our views of God have stifled our collective identity. We've gotten caught up in cultures of performance. But doing and saying what only sounds good and godly has left us devoid of His power. And we have become very tired Christians—still stuck in patterns of sin and shame.

We must return to our fiery, first love for Jesus! Following the ways of Jesus will lead us out of our lies and into His glorious life. Where all strivings cease. And where we'll find the real soul rest we seek. (Isaiah 30:15) As we allow Him to heal our hearts and lead us out of dysfunctional striving, away from emotional disconnection, He'll uncover the reality of our belonging to Him and to each other. Our thoughts and actions will align with His heart, and together we'll become His glorious dwelling place.

By communing with Him and each other according to His Spirit, proper authority will be released in great love and humility. As groups of healthy individuals and families unite—to inspire and empower each other towards health and wholeness—we'll be fully restored. For *His* goodness to be seen and known on the Earth! Kingdom communities will sustain His fullness and host His pure presence in powerful ways until Jesus returns.

Intimate Encounters

Communion

"Dear Child, you are good because I created you in My image and declared you, 'Good.' I have never expected your perfection. In truth, nothing you could ever do would make Me love you more, and nothing would ever make Me love you less. Falling short of the glorious life I've destined for you does not make me angry or disappointed with you; rather, because your value is enduring to Me, I sought you out. Jesus opened the way, so that you can get off the roller-coaster ride. We are one, just as Jesus is in Me, so you are in Him. When you fail, simply return to my embrace. Love and grace are always flowing for you. So rest in your belief in who I AM; and as you do, rivers of living water will naturally flow from within you." (John 7:38)

Prayer for Healing

"Father, You created me in Your own image. You valued me even before I saw my own value. Forgive me for allowing my negative perceptions of myself to cloud my understanding of how You see me. Since You've shown that I don't have to perform for You, I will let go of all striving. I am returning to Your embrace and receiving Your love and grace through the blood of Jesus. The truth is, nothing can ever pull me away from You. No matter what, your grace always covers me, even when I fall into sin. And so, shame has no place in me as I remain in consistent

connection with Your heart, as your beloved child. My life is now hidden in Christ. I praise You! For my guilt is all gone. I trust Your process for growing fruit in me, and I rest in the truth that there's nothing more I must do for You to be pleased with my life. Amen."

Truth Darts

- **GOD CREATED ME AND CALLED ME GOOD.**

"God saw all that he had made, and it was very good." (Genesis 1:31)

- **HE ALONE IS PERFECT, AND I STAND COMPLETE IN HIS RIGHTEOUSNESS.**

"Soak me in your laundry and I'll come out clean, scrub me and I'll have a snow-white life. Tune me in to foot-tapping songs, set these once-broken bones to dancing. Don't look too close for blemishes, give me a clean bill of health. God, make a fresh start in me, shape a Genesis week from the chaos of my life." (Psalm 51:7-10 MSG)

- **IT'S ALL ABOUT HIM, AND YET HE CALLS ME INTO HIS LIFE.**

"I have been crucified with Christ; and it is no longer I who live, but Christ lives in me; and the life which I now live in the flesh I live by faith in the Son of God, who loved me and gave Himself up for me." (Galatians 2:20)

- **BEING MY FATHER'S BELOVED CHILD IS ENOUGH FOR ME.**

"See how great a love the Father has given us, that we would be called children of God; and in fact we are. For this reason the world does not know us: because it did not know Him. Beloved, now we are children of God, and it has not appeared as yet what we will be. We know that when He appears, we will

be like Him, because we will see Him just as He is."
(1 John 3:1-2)

- **GOOD FRUIT NATURALLY COMES BY ABIDING IN CHRIST.**

"I am the vine, you are the branches; the one who remains in Me, and I in him bears much fruit, for apart from Me you can do nothing." (John 15:5

CHAPTER 7

PEOPLE PLEASING PEOPLE

*"My value comes by measuring up
to an external standard of perfection.
Pleasing others is of paramount importance."*

One year during Songkran, the largest Thai national holiday celebrated with water festivities, our whole team sat together around the dining table. We brainstormed ideas for the upcoming outreach opportunity. For three days during the holiday, families and friends would gather to celebrate and welcome the coming rainy season by throwing bowls of water everywhere. And so, our team wanted to go out and build intentional connections while also having fun with our Thai neighbors. "What's the best way to express the love of Jesus during this Songkran holiday?" we all pondered. Someone suggested handing out bottles of water. But, because water would be plentiful, I proposed expressing God's extravagant love by sharing small bottles of soda instead.

When my idea was dismissed by almost everyone on the team, my cheeks burned hot. Stunned, I wondered why my friends had outrightly disagreed with me. I felt humiliated. *Was my thought so bad that I shouldn't have even suggested it?* I lamented inwardly. Though my teammates reminded me that we all shared the same goal for the event, I felt ashamed. Dejected, I concluded something was wrong with me. I took it personally and believed my ideas were unimportant. *Maybe being different is bad. I'll never perfectly please other people, and this is proof that I'm not acceptable.*

The Lie Explained

Just like feeling rejected when my ideas weren't celebrated, some Christians are easily offended and shut down when others disagree with them. Because they feel intimidated by powerful people, they have learned to blend in with the crowd rather than confidently stand out. To share their thoughts and ideas. Like immature teenagers, many Christians have succumbed to peer pressure in their attempt to avoid rejection. Their self-confidence is shattered. And they consistently try to be in agreement with everyone around them. The pressure to live up to external, and often ambiguous, human standards of others has knotted them up inside. And so they may experience intense anxiety, desperately trying to meet others' expectations, whether real or only imagined. Perhaps they downplay their personal value and believe others' perspectives of them are most important.

And their fear of man has even caused some Christians to trust others' standards over God's own heart. Often second-guessing themselves, they wonder if they can hear His voice at all. Sadly, they doubt whether they ever have. *What is God saying? Can I really hear His voice for myself?* At times they even think God calls people with special gifts and abilities to hear Him on their behalf.

Low self-esteem has tempted many Christians away from active and obedient faith in God, too. Fear has hindered them from taking real risks with Him. It could be that God spoke, or the Holy Spirit urged them to step out in faith in a particular area in their life; and excitedly, they shared their vision. But when their ideas were met with indifference or criticism, they dismissed them as unimportant. *What is important about my God-story? Honestly, how is it any different from all the others?* Rather than being themselves in Christ, many believers have learned to mimic the sounds of influential people they admire; and in the process have lost their own voice. But, placing people on pedestals has allowed others space inside that is meant for God alone. For many Christians, people-pleasing has become an idol and is helping no one.

Truth from God's Word

The fact is, self-worth is not based on how well we follow external sets of human standards. While others' expectations of us may be good or even godly, the ability to meet them isn't where true value stems from. Simply put, people are important because we are God's chosen creation. Human value is founded upon the truth that God—who is the very essence of true love—chose to love us. In Him, we are God's "chosen people, a royal priesthood, a holy nation, God's special possession." (1 Peter 2:9)

Faith in Christ must work its way out into everyday moments and empower Christians to live in the purpose we're all created for. His reality must consistently affect how we view ourselves and how we interact. As dependence on Christ deepens, inner confidence grows. Regardless of who understands us or doesn't, and whether or not they agree, security is bolstered by remaining in His love. Rather than aiming to fit into cultural ideals, believers must realize our freedom! (Galatians 5) And we must become strengthened to step out and be *His* image-bearers.

Truly, only the intimate presence of Jesus truly satisfies the soul and sustains us. Along with the author of Psalms, each of us can fearlessly declare that "He only is my rock and my salvation, my stronghold; I shall not be shaken. On God my salvation and my glory rest; the rock of my strength, my refuge is in God." (Psalm 62:6-7)

Consequences for Disregarding the Truth

Because Christians often have an incomplete understanding of true identity in Christ, they idolize people and don't esteem each other according to how our Father does. When value is improperly placed in the thoughts and opinions of imperfect people instead of in God's words, believers become confused. And because truth grows distant and more unclear, they are led away by their fears. In confusion, they exchange the truth of God for a lie. (Romans 1:25)

Insecurity also creates trouble within relationships and institutes imbalance within the body of Christ too. By not regarding each other according to the spirit, value is awarded according to external value. And influence is assigned as we idolize names and titles. Then sadly, power becomes dangerously misappropriated among us. Worrying that we aren't enough for God or pridefully believing others aren't, we avoid addressing our differences. Instead of practicing healthy conflict resolution, we fight and bicker only to bolster our egos. Friend, can you identify with any of this?

In the attempt to fit into earthly cultures, sometimes standards are altered. And rather than boldly stand out and reform them, Christians often shrink back and settle in—overlooking how "wide and long and high and deep is the love of Christ." We fall short and fail to fully "know this love that surpasses knowledge." (Ephesians 3:18-19)

Truly, God has great purpose for His body on Earth, but the enemy often uses fear and insecurities to thwart the fulfillment of His Great Commission. The truth is, none of us has a complete understanding of who God is, and each of our perspectives is important to the whole. By believing we must all do similar works and sound the same, we limit God's intended purpose and the authority that is meant to come through His whole body. Like a puzzle requires every piece for it to become complete, Christians must not hesitate to share our gifts.

Releasing Fears Leads to Freedom

Worshipping Jesus is our remedy. Truly, believers must choose to release their fears of pleasing other people and partner with God's great love to overcome. This is how freedom from the vice of people-pleasing came for me. While I longed for acceptance, I realized that idolizing the people I admired or feared—for me, people with authority—actually kept me in bondage. A people-pleasing spirit distanced me from God and others, thereby creating a cycle of dysfunction. Once, in Thailand, God spoke to me about my addiction to pleasing others.

So, as you may remember, I grew up desperately trying to please my parents and never disappoint them. Well, they came to visit us—while I was struggling as a mother—in Thailand. And one day without Randy, we attended a large outdoor conference in Chiang Mai. We sat there, surrounded by a large crowd of people on woven mats. My children were being irritatingly loud and rambunctious, and I felt a pressure to parent them perfectly—in accordance with the way my parents expected. But It was a trap. And when I caved and punished my children out of fear of what my parents were thinking (whether actual or not), I felt horrible. Immediately, I became aware of the many times I had acted out of a people-pleasing spirit. *Father. I am so sorry. I've settled with a fear of man rather than trusting You. I believe that you will teach me how to parent in the best way for me and my children.*

Encountering God that day didn't feel great, but He opened my eyes to the truth. His perfect love rushed into all the places where my insecurity had tried to please others, to feel better about myself. Usually, acting on God's words rather than my feelings required bravery. Especially when His truth seemed to be in opposition with what I was taught or when people around me disapproved. But as I adjusted my heart to walk according to faith, inner security grew and even became more natural. While I am still a work in progress, I no longer undervalue my true self-worth and unique purpose. I'm not bound to a people-pleasing spirit anymore, and I've grown more confident to stand in my own space. Even when I'm misunderstood or disagreed with, it's still possible to be myself and present my ideas!

Being responsible for ourselves frees us to love others better, too. The truth is, every person is uniquely created to fulfill the purposes of God in the very special ways that only they can. And freedom instigates more healing. When God's love becomes the foundation in all things, people are healed and set free—which transforms relationships. Instead of taking up offenses when we're misunderstood—as I was when my Coke idea wasn't adopted by the team—healing allows us to see and hear others, without our false, pain filters. Just like Jesus stepped out and didn't allow pain to keep him from living victoriously, we are capable of remaining in His love even when faced with rejection—as He was. Truly, locking eyes with Jesus and encountering Him face-to-face restores us from the inside out.

Intimate Encounters

COMMUNION

"Dear Child, 'Do not fear, for I have redeemed you; I have called you by name; you are Mine!' (Isaiah 43:1) I have built you to know me, to really know me. And, my steady presence in your everyday life is your sure and strong foundation. That, my child, is where your confidence can become solid. As you learn that nothing can ever separate you from My love, you will grow steady, being swayed by nothing, not even your own mistakes. These will no longer distract you away from Me. Your position is forever in Christ, and I have created you to live powerfully, aware of the authority you have to walk in victory."

PRAYER FOR HEALING

"Father, I don't want to live in agreement with fear or insecurity anymore. The people-pleasing can never provide the confidence I was created to know and experience in You alone. I acknowledge that in the past, I have idolized the opinions of man. Please restore my heart and mind so that I can trust Your steady love and acceptance as my sure foundation. Give me a clear vision of myself, healed and whole. Reveal to me how I am a piece of the whole, meant for creating healthy kingdom cultures within my sphere of influence. Amen."

Truth Darts

- **I WILL SERVE NO OTHER GOD BUT YOU!**

"You shall have no other gods before Me. You shall not make for yourself an idol, or any likeness of what is in Heaven above or on the earth beneath, or in the water under the earth. You shall not worship them nor serve them; for I, the Lord your God, am a jealous God, inflicting the punishment of the fathers on the children, on the third and the fourth generations of those who hate Me." (Exodus 20:3-5)

- **CONFIDENCE IS KNOWING THAT GOD'S PRESENCE IS MY FOUNDATION.**

"Be strong and courageous, do not be afraid or in dread of them, for the Lord your God is the One who is going with you. He will not desert you or abandon you." (Deuteronomy 31:6)

- **NOTHING WILL EVER SEPARATE ME FROM HIS LOVE.**

"For I am convinced that neither death, nor life, nor angels, nor principalities, nor things present, nor things to come, nor powers, nor height, nor depth, nor any other created thing will be able to separate us from the love of God that is in Christ Jesus our Lord." (Romans 8:38-39)

- **I AM FOREVER SECURE IN MY FATHER'S SURE AND STEADY LOVE.**

"For as many as the promises of God are, in Him they are yes; therefore through Him also is our Amen to the glory of God through us. Now He who

establishes us with you in Christ and anointed us is God, who also sealed us and gave us the Spirit in our hearts as a pledge." (1 Corinthians 1:20-22)

- **I WILL LIVE FROM MY POSITION IN CHRIST.**

  "[God] ... made us alive together with Christ (by grace you have been saved), and raised us up with Him, and seated us with Him in the heavenly places in Christ Jesus." (Ephesians 2:5-6)

CHAPTER 8

VULNERABILITY? YIKES.

*"Vulnerability reveals weakness.
No one truly understands me, so I must
carry the weight of my weakness alone."*

A few summers ago, my graduating class gathered to celebrate our twenty-year reunion. Leading up to the event, my excitement intensified as I expectantly prepared to interact with friends I hadn't seen since high school. You see, though I was well-liked, I didn't believe so. Back then, a severe inferiority complex had locked me up inside, leaving me feeling intimidated and self-conscious. Though I was on fire for Jesus and wanted all my friends to experience His love, I mostly kept Him to myself. Vulnerability felt scary, so I protected myself by maintaining an emotionally distant exterior.

But, since that long-ago season, I had experienced much inner healing through Jesus. And so, I was convinced, *This is my chance! There's nothing left to fear or prove. Father, empower me to shine Your light.* Incredibly, I was able to leap out of my comfort zone and reveal my authentic self. Through loud laughter and raucous reminiscing with people who never truly knew me during high school, God revealed His deep love. Previously distanced friends were given the opportunity to encounter Jesus and experience freedom for themselves, too.

The Lie Explained

In the same way I hid myself throughout high school, people, sadly, often aren't transparent with each other because they fear being judged wrongly or getting hurt. They believe the lie that revealing their heart is dangerous. Instead of living freely without pretense, Christians, too, paste on Sunday smiles and pretend to be fine. Because of pain, perhaps they hide, even from trustworthy friends. I know I have. *It's just too risky. My vulnerability could end up being used against me,* I told myself. But lack of vulnerability distances Christians from God, disconnects us from healthy relationships, and diminishes the glorious light we're all meant to shine out.

Most people don't like appearing weak. And so they hide their faults until they feel strong or capable. Only then do they make themselves seen and known. *When I'm good enough, I'll be authentic about what's going on inside.* Like I did, they struggle to open up and allow others to know them—always keeping their guard up. *Being vulnerable feels dangerous.* Constantly, they cover their real thoughts and feelings, hoping their inner struggles aren't showing through. Although Christians desire true intimacy, inner isolation has become a close friend of many. It's possible that by keeping to themselves, they've separated themselves from the very wisdom and support others could offer them on the journey.

Some Christians have a past they aren't proud of. Though they have repented of their sin and are walking a new path, they still worry they'll be judged according to their failures. And so, while they're authentic enough to share a brief testimony, they still withhold parts and pieces. They tell their story in just the right ways for others to approve. It's true, Jesus rescued all of us from sin and shame, and His transformative power has made us whole. But for some, being real about it seems impossible. *That was such a long time ago, and my sin is completely removed.* They remind Him. *Telling my story now seems pointless and unnecessarily painful.* Even though they're free from the mess of the past, they idolize their new reputation.

Other Christians don't seem to have a negative past at all. They're thriving in relationship with God, and inwardly they're excited about it! Yet, they dampen their passion in public because they're afraid of shining "too bright." Perhaps pride has gotten in their way of fully expressing authentic love for the Lord. They replace real intimacy for knowledge or good deeds and label their stoicism as "spiritual maturity." While their subdued outward appearance keeps them comfortably content within their Christian bubbles, quite possibly it also thwarts their growth. And it could hinder them from participating in the grand adventures God has invited them into with Him! Maybe something about this sounds familiar to you?

Truth from God's Word

Currently, many Christians don't experience God's real and intimate presence in their everyday lives to the degree that they easily engage in authentic, heart-to-heart connections with others. And believing that they shouldn't be vulnerable or can't is a dangerous lie. The truth is, vulnerability is a valuable tool God uses to unlock greater realms of His glory within our personal lives; and to thereby create healthy cultures capable of sustaining His kingdom on Earth. And so, we must desire grace, which is available for losing the facades and living unmasked. His abundant life will flow more freely on Earth as we practice fearless vulnerability with God and each other.

According to Merriam-Webster, vulnerability is defined as "capable of being physically or emotionally wounded." In mothering six children over the years, I've learned one thing for certain: babies are extremely vulnerable. Born naked and needy, they are dependent on others to meet their basic needs for survival. Clearly, babies fit the definition. Interestingly, God honored vulnerability by presenting Himself in this very way, such that He came to Earth in the form of a human baby. To become one of us. He purposefully placed Himself in a dangerously dependent situation, entrusting Himself to humanity.

Jesus was born into the most vulnerable of human conditions, and He also chose authentic childlikeness as His lifestyle. Throughout His earthly life, Jesus chose to live capable of being wounded, both physically and emotionally. He was by far the most spiritually mature human being who ever lived, and yet He taught His disciples that to be great is to first become small. Jesus did that! His friends asked Him, "Who then is greatest in the kingdom of heaven?" and He replied, "Whoever will humble himself like this child, he is the greatest in the kingdom of heaven." (Matthew 18:1-4)

Not only did Jesus preach how entering the kingdom of God requires vulnerability, but He also practiced it: "He got up from the meal, took off his outer clothing, and wrapped a towel around his waist. After that, he poured water into a basin and began to wash his disciples' feet, drying them with the towel that was wrapped around him." (John 13:4-5) Jesus set the example, showing us how to live. He trusted God and served His friends, all the while knowing they would soon abandon Him. Not long after His beautiful act of service, He was betrayed by Judas and denied by Peter. He was doubted by Thomas and mis-understood by most of the disciples. Even the well-studied Pharisees and teachers of the Law had no idea who He was. Yet, throughout His life, Jesus remained emotionally present—even when He felt hurt, again and again. How's that for vul-nerability?

He knew the secret. And this is a key for us, too: by living simply reliant on the Father with childlike authenticity, He remained steadfast. He had one mission, and He lived it no matter who understood Him and who didn't. Ours is no more complicated than His. By openly revealing the Father's love, He introduced a whole new king-dom and altered Earth's culture forever; such that, greatness equals humility. And often, humility requires vulnerability. Jesus's vulnerability was a tool, showing the whole world *how* to love even through suffering. Truly, the culmination of His great love was revealed as He hung on the cross, his pain exposed for all to see: "Father, forgive them; for they do not know what they are doing." (Luke 23:34)

Consequences for Disregarding the Truth

It's no lie that living transparently like Jesus and expressing authenticity in relationships does carry risks. But, although vulnerability is dan-gerous, comfortably stoic is actually more so! In fact, there are grave consequences for choosing isolation. It's like being in a crowded room but still feeling lonely. In truth, the heart posture of emotional isolation hurts worse than being physically alone. Suffering silently perpetuates many problems and complicates relationships, too. For loneliness, deep sadness, and prolonged grief turn us into easy targets for the enemy. We read in Ecclesiastes, "Two are better than one because they have a good return for their labor; for if either of them falls, the one will lift up his companion. But woe to the one who falls when there is not another to lift him up! Furthermore, if two lie down together they keep warm, but how can one be warm alone? And if one can overpower him who is alone, two can resist him. A cord of three strands is not quickly torn apart." (Ecclesiastes 4:9-12)

Spiritual pride is another potential consequence of remaining emotionally isolated. If we prioritize external looks over revealing the truth of our hearts, our reputations may have become idols. Though desirable because they reveal true character, good reputations were never meant to be worshipped. In fact, Jesus called out the religious leaders of His day, "For you are like whitewashed tombs which on the outside appear beautiful, but inside they are full of dead men's bones and all uncleanness. So you too, outwardly appear righteous to people, but inwardly you are full of hypocrisy and lawlessness." (Matthew 23:27-28) It's possible that by withholding parts and pieces from our God-stories, Christians allow spiritual pride to set us up for greater spiritual and moral failure.

Vulnerability isn't neat and tidy, though, is it? In fact, transparency is often painful and messy. But, breakthroughs come through brokenness. And, trying to protect our reputations by patching up and covering the broken places stifles the light and warmth of Jesus that's meant to shine through us and be shared with the world! In essence, self-preservation actually hinders the expansion of God's glorious kingdom upon the Earth. In opting for the safety of our comfort zones over humble breakthroughs, we will never realize the fullness our Father dreams for His family. And isn't that our goal?

Growth Through Vulnerability

The truth is, the desire to belong—to be noticed and needed and important—is how we've been created! In the same way we are invited into the deep unity of the Father, Son, and Holy Spirit, we are also created for deep and vulnerable connections with others. To grow into the body of Christ He intends us to be, we must return to the very simple and childlike way of Jesus. As we allow Him, the Holy Spirit will free us from hiding behind our good reputations. Instead, we'll learn to value truth in the innermost places. And vulnerability within our relationships with each other and amongst our faith communities will also grow, so that more of His abundant life can be sustained among us on Earth as it is in Heaven.

Believers must break down the walls of pride and prejudice that have separated us, because living and thriving within healthy cultures is how we discover who we are, how we belong, and what we're created to do. And we must grow in our trust and interdependence. Scripture provides a practical example of how vulnerability produces healing: "Is anyone among you suffering? Then he must pray. Is anyone cheerful? He is to sing praises. Is anyone among you sick? Then he must call for the elders of the church and they are to pray over him, anointing him with oil in the name of the Lord; and the prayer of faith will restore the one who is sick, and the Lord will raise him up, and if he has committed sins, they will be forgiven him. Therefore, confess your sins to one another, and pray for one another so that you may be healed. A prayer of a righteous person, when it is brought about, can accomplish much." (James 5:13-16)

And so, here I am, sharing my God-story with you. Several years ago, we had recently returned from living nearly seven years overseas in Thailand, where we were part of a small missionary team. In that remote region, there weren't many other Christian families; so as a wife and young mother, I often felt isolated and mostly unsupported. But now, here I was, back in the States. Though, I wasn't the same person I had been when we left, and most of our friends had moved on, too. So, I was feeling alone, again. There wasn't much interest in our overseas experiences, and no one seemed to understand my desire for reciprocal heart-to-heart connections. *Is some-*

thing wrong with me, I wondered. *Am I too late in life to develop real and lasting friendships with depth and true value?* Though we were back in America and surrounded by lots of people, I was lonely. We were "home," but my heart felt lost.

We'd been deeply hurt in church, but that is exactly where God led us. Out of our self-protective comfort zones and back into difficult heart spaces. He provided people to stand in proxy and called on me to forgive. Was it easy? Nope. Was it comfortable opening my heart back up and being misunderstood? Not at all. Did I get hurt again? Definitely. In fact, a lot. *God, why does it hurt to forgive? Must I really learn to love again?* I didn't want to open myself up and be vulnerable *again.* But, as I forgave the people who had misjudged me and my family, God healed my heart and gave me a new compassion for people. Through it, I realized how many others also feel lonely and isolated—how all of us long for real face-to-face and heart-to-heart connections with each other.

All of us must learn to express ourselves as Jesus did. Friend, He is calling you out, too! Out of your comfort zone and into deeper truth encounters with Him and others. Our mission isn't to stay safe but rather to remain in His love, similarly to when I jumped out of my comfort zone at my high school reunion several years ago. Instead of staying emotionally isolated behind walls of self-preservation, we can partner with Him and practice being real.

Intimate Encounters

COMMUNION

"Dear Child, you will forever belong with Me, and nothing can ever separate you from My love. Therefore, you can let go of trying to make yourself great and simply become childlike in your trust. I know there are times when you have felt hurt and hidden yourself away; but with your trust, I will stand on your behalf. You needn't fear trusting Me, for I am your vindicator. I will protect you when you open your heart to others. Because I have shown you the way to remain secure in my love, I will empower you also to love others in the same way. Choosing to live with an authentic, open heart is a gift, dear child. Never hold back from shining brightly. For as you trust Me, your simple vulnerability will become a wide platform for others to experience My Light."

PRAYER FOR HEALING

"Father, thank You, for I belong with You forever, and nothing can ever separate me from Your deep love. Not only can I trust You, but You gave me people to walk alongside in this journey of life. I'm not alone. Help me be like Jesus, through all of my humanity and pain and heartache within relationships. I depend on Jesus for my emotional security. Help me be childlike and consistently open with others. I don't have to fear being vulnerable with others.

Every person ever placed in my life is valuable. Thank you for the lessons I've learned in walking with each one. As You continue to heal my emotional wounds,

I trust You to shine through the places of my healed brokenness. These spaces are for Your glory.
I trust You to bring people into my life at just the right times for my growth and development, and to provide opportunities for me to share Your goodness with them. Give me discernment to know people and situations according to the Holy Spirit, and grant me wisdom to understand as You do. I believe my vulnerability is a gift, and I will trust Your guidance to know when and how to share it. Amen."

Truth Darts

- **I BELONG TO GOD FOREVER.**

  "Know that the Lord is God. It is he who made us, and we are his; we are his people, the sheep of his pasture." (Psalm 100:3)

- **GOD IS MY VINDICATOR.**

  "Judge me, Lord my God, according to Your righteousness, and do not let them rejoice over me." (Psalm 35:24)

- **I CAN BE OBEDIENT TO JESUS AND BECOME CHILDLIKE.**

  "Truly I say to you, unless you change and become like children, you will not enter the kingdom of heaven." (Matthew 18:3)

- **JESUS REMAINED IN LOVE, EVEN AMID HIS PAIN, SO I CAN TOO.**

  "But Jesus was saying, 'Father, forgive them; for they do not know what they are doing.' " (Luke 23:34)

- **VULNERABILITY OPENS OPPORTUNITIES FOR MORE HEALING.**

  "Therefore, confess your sins to one another, and pray for one another so that you may be healed. A prayer of a righteous person, when it is brought about, can accomplish much." (James 5:16)

CHAPTER 9

MINISTRY ROLES AND TITLES

"Ministry is the special appointment of a select, powerful few. If I don't have a role or title, my work is less important."

Our family loves good Thai fruit. Recently, after dropping our daughter off at the airport for one of her grand adventures, we stopped at our favorite market to buy some exotic varieties unavailable at our regular grocery store.

When we arrived home, I showed the boys how to peel a lychee fruit. Pondering, one of the youngest asked, "Mom, if this fruit hadn't been picked yet, would it have gotten bigger and turned into a durian?" Now, in case you're unfamiliar, lychee is a round fruit, a bit smaller than a golf ball, with bumpy, jewel-toned ridges on the thin outer skin. They taste refreshingly smooth and sweet. Durian, however, are very large fruits with green, spiky outer shells. Their yellow flesh is quite stinky, tasting something like a combination of bananas, garlic, and wet socks. The two fruits are absolutely nothing alike, except that both are grown in Southeast Asia.

His question struck me, though, and I immediately knew there was a lesson in it for all of us. I pondered for a moment, "Hmmm, do you think a full-grown strawberry would ever get as big as a watermelon?" I teased. "Or, what about a blueberry looking like a pineapple?" And, we laughed.

Obviously, a mature lychee fruit will never get as big as a durian. And that is a good thing, because lychee isn't valued based on its shape or size, or durian-ness. Rather, it's prized specifically because it's a lychee.

The Lie Explained

Similar to judging lychee against durian, people aren't meant to be judged against other people. And outward expressions aren't to be compared with those of others, either. What does this mean? Often, Christians are guilty of measuring themselves and others against human standards, especially within church cultures. This is evidenced by how achievement is applauded and value placed on what's biggest and best.

Sometimes, people with ministry titles are deemed most important. *They are the only ones called into ministry*. And those with large followings or important roles are granted as more valuable in God's kingdom. Charismatic leaders—with pronounced outward expressions—are often awarded more societal influence, even at times chosen more for their personality than by God's appointment.

I had bought into the ugly lie. *My passport will finally make my life count for Jesus,* I thought. *And becoming a missionary to an exotic, remote destination is my ticket to becoming somebody great for God.* I was a new mom when our family lived as missionaries in Thailand. And several times, when our team journeyed along dusty dirt roads to minister in the villages, I remained at home, praying from a distance and caring for our young children. "This work doesn't seem valuable, God. My life isn't making any spiritual impact at all," I cried out to Him. Because of the high value I placed on overt outward expressions, sadly, I ranked my own work as less important and wasted precious moments.

Like me, many Christians understand Jesus's command to be the salt of the Earth and the light of the world, and may even receive prophetic words concerning what they're called to do for God's kingdom. (Matthew 5:13-16) But they get stuck there. They believe that doing God's work requires earning a certain degree or carrying a particular, important title—or being noticed by someone who does. Somehow, they envisioned their lives would be bigger and better than their current circumstances. And so they're stuck waiting for some ministry role to manifest before they can be impactful. Perhaps they even grow hopeless or resentful with their situation. *Someday, maybe when I'm more spiritually mature, then I'll be an important leader,* they conclude. But, like I did as a young mom, they've disqualified themselves from living an impactful life for God right where they are!

Truth from God's Word

"Ministry" is a confusing term for many, perhaps because it has often been used to perpetuate separation between those who have titles or positions and those who do not. Granted, some people operate as ordained ministers, and some are unordained. But, the truth is, all of us are called to minister! And, every single one of us is chosen and appointed for specific and very important tasks. (Ephesians 1:4-5, Ephesians 2:10) But first, we must come to a proper understanding of the term. So, what is ministry, anyway?

As defined by Merriam-Webster, the word "ministry" refers to "the office, duties, or functions of a minister, the body of ministers of religion."

This definition often implies that only those with particular roles are given the responsibility of ministry. And since most church cultures reflect this definition, it must be addressed. As we continue to shed lies about who we are and mature into the people of God, I propose that a better definition of "ministry" could prove beneficial. For the sake of our understanding, we'll refer to ministry as "the unique expressions that flow from a pure understanding and application of one's identity in Christ."

The truth is, people are created uniquely, and therefore, each one should be appointed specifically, according to God's careful wisdom. "For we are His workmanship, created in Christ Jesus for good works, which God prepared beforehand so that we would walk in them." (Ephesians 2:10) Ministry is an outflow of our identity in Christ and is meant to occur naturally as we remain in Him. Since real and lasting fruit can only come by maintaining a vibrant relationship with Jesus, only work that is done *with Him* will last. Anything accomplished apart from Him is not real or permanent. Period. No matter how good our outward expressions look or how many followers we have, if we're not connected to Jesus, it's not authentic ministry. He said, "Remain in Me, and I in you. Just as the branch cannot bear fruit of itself but must remain in the vine, so neither can you unless you remain in Me. I am the vine, you are the branches; the one who remains in Me, and I in him bears much fruit, for apart from Me you can do nothing." (John 15:4-5)[1]

---

1   Much has been written on the topic of specific spiritual "ministry" gifts that exist among the family of God for the building up of the saints. Thankfully, God delegates positions within His church for the sake of organization. And although it is not my intention to devalue the importance of the topic, that conversation will not be addressed here. If you have further interest, please explore Ephesians 4, Revive the Way resources, and other related books.

Consequences for Disregarding the Truth

Obviously, as believers, we want our lives to be fruitful, and we want to make an impact in God's kingdom. But, measuring the value of our fruit by inappropriate methods negatively affects all of us. Many Christians have lost sight of what God values and have built paradigms, accordingly. Though in truth, "God does not see as man sees, since man looks at the outward appearance, but the Lord looks at the heart." (1 Samuel 16:7) Believing ministry is the work of a select few who carry specific, important titles has ultimately limited the impact every single believer is meant to have in God's kingdom. And sadly, by esteeming each other according to ranks set by the standards of man, systems have been set that praise the prestigious and look down on those appearing powerless.

Though none of us wants to admit we believe that certain titles and roles are most important, it's often how we operate within Christian communities. I wonder, what religious cultures we've built, tended, and endorsed that God hasn't?

Ultimately, since prowess has been prized—and servanthood seems shameful—Christians are striving for significance rather than simply pursuing thriving personal and intimate relationships with Jesus. They've lost their first love and haven't learned to rest in His finished work, therefore missing out on the joyful process. They measure success by the names and numbers of people they've shared Jesus with, rather than by truly engaging with Him in their everyday lives. Spiritual "rank" has even been idolized so that many believers judge each other improperly— by what they do, rather than by who they are in Christ. Misunderstanding what true ministry is has sometimes even created a competitive culture, at times placing an unhealthy wedge between leadership and laity. And misunderstanding what true ministry is has sabotaged the health of authentic Christian communities. But just like judging lychee against durian, it is futile to measure ourselves against each other.

Ministry: Jesus, Our Best Example

As believers, we must understand that Jesus is our best ministry example. Our specific expressions are meant to stem from our identity in Christ— the unique ways we communicate His love in the world as only we can. All of us are called! Rather than requiring a role or title, ministry is simply the overflow of our relationship with Him. Therefore, our Christian cultural ideals must shift to reflect a more godly approach to ministry.

We bear His Name. Thus, we must demonstrate who He is properly and minister in the way He did! Since His life is our pattern, learning and receiving directly from Him is the simplest way to accurately emulate His life. Just as Jesus knew He was chosen by God and boldly expressed His earthly mission, so it is the Father's plan for every one of us. (Luke 4:18-19) Each of us must trust we've been chosen before our birth and were created for a unique purpose. None of us came by chance. (Isaiah 43:1)

And we must agree with God that all of us are destined for His purposes. Whether caring for people on the job, volunteering at the local shelter, or raising a family, everyone's work is valuable. In the same way Jesus gave His life, we have nothing to defend or prove; we can empty ourselves of pride and ego. Like Him, we can give our lives to God and serve others through His pure and radical love. He emptied Himself, and so can we. He carried great authority and yet expressed His love through humility, and so we must also minister by our servanthood. As we work unto the Lord and not for man, we have His encouragement to: "work heartily, as for the Lord and not for people, knowing that it is from the Lord." (Colossians 3:23-24) It's less about *what* we do and more about *who* we are doing it for and *why*.

Truly, the gospel is meant to spread out and have an impact on the culture around us. Just like Jesus commissioned His disciples, we are also empowered by His Holy Spirit to "go, therefore, and make disciples of all the nations." (Matthew 28:19) Each of us is called into ministry, though it's up to us to discover the unique purpose we are created for. Each of our expressions is needed and must flow from a true understanding and application of our identity in Christ.

Dear one, do you know you are chosen and appointed to bear good fruit? Truly, roles and titles mean absolutely nothing in His eyes. And trying to be who we're not is like trying to produce fruit we're not meant to bear. Do you believe you've been called and commissioned by His Holy Spirit to take His message of good news out to a lost and broken generation? He's anointed you with a special message of reconciliation for this hour. Perhaps you've questioned whether the Lord is speaking, since what He's saying sounds uncomfortably different, non-religious even. But, will you dare to patiently walk out His purposes for you, even if it means walking alone in the beginning? Can the Father trust you with His special mission? Be encouraged! Rise up in the pure authority of Christ in you and powerfully minister His love, in the way that only you can.

Intimate Encounters

COMMUNION

"Dear Child, you are chosen. For such a time as this, I have called you and appointed you to bear good and godly fruit. While you can do nothing apart from remaining in Me, the truth is that as you actively remain in Me, you will surely bear fruit—and much of it! It is My desire that you do so, because that is how My Father is glorified. In fact, 'Your light must shine before people in such a way that they may see your good works.' (John 15:8, Matthew 5:16) Just as I sent out the apostles, so also I am sending you to be My ambassador. God is making His appeal through you. (2 Corinthians 5:20) As you minister in love, I offer reconciliation through your surrendered life. Surely, I am with you wherever you go!"

PRAYER FOR HEALING

"Father, You have chosen me and called me by my name. As I go about the life work You have given to me, I rest knowing that You have ordained me for the tasks at hand, according to my identity as Your beloved child. I bear Your Name, and I trust that I am empowered to love as Jesus did. Not only have You appointed me to bear good fruit as I abide in Jesus, but You said I would bear much fruit, too. And, it is only for Your glory that I do. Whether or not I carry a significant position or title is not important. Rather, I trust that my ministry is unique and valuable to Your plan of redemption for the whole world. No matter what roles I operate within at any given time, I believe Your Spirit is upon me, for You

have anointed me to proclaim good news to the poor, recovery of sight to the blind, and freedom to the oppressed. You have said that as I shine brightly, Your abundant life will be seen and known by others. You are sending me as an ambassador of Heaven, to accomplish Your purposes on Earth while I'm here. Thank You for the privilege to join You in the work of reconciliation. Amen."

Truth Darts

- **I AM CHOSEN.**

  "But you are a chosen people, a royal priesthood, a holy nation, a people for God's own possession, so that you may proclaim the excellencies of Him who has called you out of darkness into His marvelous light." (1 Peter 2:9)

- **I AM APPOINTED BY GOD TO BEAR GOOD FRUIT.**

  "You did not choose Me but I chose you, and appointed you that you would go and bear fruit, and that your fruit would remain, so that whatever you ask of the Father in My name He may give to you." (John 15:16)

- **I CAN LET MY LIGHT SHINE BRIGHTLY.**

  "Your light must shine before people in such a way that they may see your good works, and glorify your Father who is in heaven. (Matthew 5:16)

- **I AM A MINISTER OF RECONCILIATION.**

  "All this is from God, who reconciled us to himself through Christ and gave us the ministry of reconciliation: that God was reconciling the world to himself in Christ, not counting people's sins against them. And he has committed to us the message of reconciliation. We are therefore Christ's ambassadors, as though God were making his appeal through us. We implore you on Christ's behalf: Be reconciled to God." (2 Corinthians 5:18-20)

- **I AM SENT.**

"Jesus summoned His twelve disciples and gave them authority over unclean spirits, to cast them out, and to heal every disease and every sickness." (Matthew 10:1)

"Then Jesus came to them and said, 'All authority in heaven and on earth has been given to me. Therefore go and make disciples of all nations, baptizing them in the name of the Father and of the Son and of the Holy Spirit, and teaching them to obey everything I have commanded you. And surely I am with you always, to the very end of the age.' " (Matthew 28:18-20)

CHAPTER 10

ABUNDANT LIFE: WHAT'S IT FOR, ANYWAY?

*"Never doubt God's mighty power to work
in you and accomplish all this. He will
achieve infinitely more than your greatest
request, your most unbelievable dream,
and exceed your wildest imagination!"*

Ephesians 3:20 TPT

Once, during a break from language school,
our family took the bumpy overnight
train ride from Bangkok to the northeast
region of Thailand, where our team was serving.
That weekend, all of us gathered excitedly around
the computer for a Skype phone call with teammates who were on furlough in the States. Lynn
began, "You know, I have something I'd like to
share with you all," and he proceeded to tell us

that he was recently diagnosed with a progressive neurodegenerative disease. But he wasn't fearful or worried. God had led him to a scripture passage that promised, "This sickness will not end in death. No, it is for God's glory so that God's Son may be glorified through it." (John 11:4 NIV)

We nodded our heartfelt agreement. And though we didn't know what lay ahead, over the next months all of us believed and prayed, and prayed and believed, that Lynn's body would be healed. Resurrected even. And that the Thai people might recognize God's great power through the whole experience. We dug into the scriptures, and we wrestled with His promises. *God, are You really as good as we think You are? And can we really ask for that?* Our questions didn't disappear but led us deeper into the Father's heart. In time, the focus of our faith shifted from trusting Him for particular outcomes to believing in His true character. Our trust in God broke our hearts wide open. Though Lynn passed into his heavenly life, he inspired many people to dream big! And we know that God is not finished with his story.

Over the years since then, God has consistently breathed quiet confirmations I've known for most of my life, "These are holy moments to be alive." The truth is, every believer has a calling to fulfill with God, a race to run. As His holy people, the assignment is as it always was, to "be fruitful and multiply. Fill the earth and govern it." (Genesis 1:28 NLT) Every Christian is created to faithfully participate with Him in revealing His kingdom, to devotedly occupy the Earth until He returns! Surely, many precious people—faith-filled men and women just like Lynn—believed and prayed, and prayed and believed, for days like now. They went on before us and joined the great cloud of witnesses, cheering all of us on towards God and His great purposes!

Truth from God's Word

I wonder. *Are Christians fully aware of why we're here? Do we understand the corporate purpose of being part of God's family?* Throughout history, periods of refreshment referred to as *revivals* have inspired people to seek the things of God, so that they "see, hear, feel and taste the powers of the world to come."[1] And these moments are wonderfully special—when God's Spirit breaks through—and lives are transformed. But, unfortunately, the impacts of revival have typically been short-lived and concentrated to specific locations; as believers generally haven't effectively stewarded God's work within their own hearts. In truth, corporate revival must be sustained on the Earth through individuals.

And Jesus showed us the way. Since He taught His disciples to "seek first His kingdom and His righteousness," then He wants us to seek first His kingdom, too. In the same way He prayed for God's kingdom to come and His will to be done

---

1	John Wesley, "Journal," Jackson, I: 251; III: 49 from https://oxford-institute.org/wp-content/uploads/2018/11/2018-10-bounds.pdf

on Earth as it is in Heaven, so must we. Not only are we called to believe and pray, and pray and believe, we are to partner *with* Him daily. How does He intend for His reality to become ours?

First, when we truly understand Jesus's words about the kingdom of God, our lives are forever altered; we realize that His kingdom is truly all about Him. And so seeking Him means being completely caught up in His life rather than expecting Him to be caught up in ours. By understanding Him rightly, our focus shifts away from demanding our own outcomes and towards trusting His character.

And second, believers must remember that not only are we forever redeemed from our great Fall, but we are also seated with Christ in glorious union forever. (Ephesians 2:5-10) While our physical bodies are planted here, we are spiritual sons and daughters of God first and foremost. And so, our freedom in Christ is just the beginning of our great inheritance. Remaining in Him means becoming like Jesus on the Earth. Jesus said that His kingdom would be detected by His powerful presence among us. (Luke 17:20)

Surrendering to the Holy Spirit

Because His kingdom is present wherever He reigns, surrender is our key to accessing it. By receiving His love and then responding through humble obedience, we express Him by acting in accordance with His very ways. As we enthrone Jesus, we occupy ground in the spiritual realm as well as within our everyday moments. Therefore, our one simple desire must be crowning Him "Lord" of every area of our lives. As Jesus is enthroned over our circumstances—acting in love even when misunderstood, offering grace even when hurt—His heavenly jurisdiction is released. For "our struggle is not against flesh and blood, but against the rulers, against the powers, against the world forces of this darkness, against the spiritual forces of wickedness in the heavenly places." (Ephesians 6:12) By standing firm in our faith, His dominion is established over spiritual darkness, and ground is gained for His kingdom in the very spheres we enter.

This reality is intended to be manifested physically, too. God has called each one of us ambassadors from His heavenly kingdom, and Christ is making His appeal through us. The very God who orders time and space handpicked each one of us for life on Earth at such a time as this, to be ministers of His reconciliation. (2 Corinthians 5:19-20) And so, He destined us for dreams and promises that will only come about as we surrender and participate with Him—here and now. Living aware of His Holy Spirit awakens us to believe for all Jesus promised. In fact, when Jesus returned to the Father, He promised them a Helper. He told His friends that because He was going away, the Holy Spirit would come upon them, and they would do even greater works than He! (John 14:12, 16-17)

If this all seems unfathomable, that's because

it is. But, Jesus said all things are possible with God. (Matthew 19:26) Since we haven't yet seen the full actualization of Jesus's prayer, portraying it can be challenging, except to use prophetic language. And so, as one of my sons recently encouraged me, I'll share honestly from the outset where my heart is: I'm here, dreaming with God, of all He has in store for us!

Abundant Life Expressed Personally

Throughout the course of this book we've taken lies seriously. Why have we been so tough on our beliefs and understanding where they're from? Because believing lies has kept the body of Christ comfortably content and distracted from contending for the fullness of His life that we are truly designed for. And getting rid of every "obstacle and the sin which so easily entangles us," creates more capacity to carry the full weight of God's glorious kingdom within us—to be filled up and overflowing!

God's gift of grace completely releases us from the grip of guilt so that now we are empowered to forgive others—and ourselves, too. We're no longer tied to mistakes from our past. Fear has been eradicated, its power gone forever! The walls of self-protection can finally fall. The filters we used to bolster our self-images aren't necessary anymore; we are free to express ourselves authentically with God and others. And our humble vulnerability is the very platform He'll use for sharing His good news with the world.

No pretense, just pure love. We don't need titles to practice powerful Christian living. For spiritual authority isn't awarded; it's stewarded—by remaining in the vine. (John 15:4)

For me, believing and praying for resurrection life to come forth within my friend's body was a real wake-up call. Before then, I hadn't ever dreamed with God for all He wanted to do on the earth. *You want me to ask what, God? Is that even something a Christian can pray for?* Honestly, I didn't believe Him for seemingly impossible things. Nor did I understand that my mission is to do exactly as Jesus did upon the earth. But, when I was willing to face Him with my questions, my doubts, and my fears, He traded them with His truth. Where I was unsure, now I know. Though we didn't see our friend's physical body raised, deep inside I am confident that one day we will! *God, I trust You to do big things as we continue believing and praying, and praying and believing.*

As Spirit-filled believers, all of us must dream big and believe we're called to do the things Jesus said we would! Revival sparks are fanned into flame as each of us brings our part—such that others are inspired, too. We can pray in faith, and we can give to nearby ministries and global missions. And we can serve by *going*, near or far, and sharing God's good news! God has been consistently building a family of faith-filled people. He's been preparing the earth to fully receive her King of glory. Truly, a faith-filled network is necessary for sustaining what is coming soon. Just as John the Baptist understood who he was and the importance of the times in which he lived, we must also discern the spiritual seasons of our lifetime. In the same way he knew that he was a "voice of one calling out in the wilderness," each of us must be about our Father's business—boldly standing out—preparing the way for Jesus! (Mark 1:3, Matthew 3:2) And He is coming soon.

Abundant Life Expressed Corporately

Not only does our Father desire for each of us to encounter freedom and wholeness on a personal level, but He longs for a healthy, connected family of people who pray as one—who dream and participate with Him to bring about His purposes on the earth while we actively await His return. Together the whole body of Christ is meant to shine with the fullness of His glory in ways that only a family can. Therefore, our corporate focus must shift away from keeping up outward appearances and towards strengthening interpersonal relationships, so that the foundations of our faith become strong and truly healthy.

As I became brutally honest regarding my mistakes and took full responsibility for my own messes, others in my life are following my lead. And in the same way that God's inner work within my heart spread its way into our family's relationships, so the whole family of God is intended for large-scale freedom and restoration, too! *Father, help us to learn new ways of being vulnerable and communicating without pretense or passivity. As*

You teach us, we will learn to practice sharing truth with love and grace.

As every believer takes personal responsibility for mistakes, fears will be released—and conflict won't seem as scary. We'll understand that our unity is not synonymous with same-ness; we'll come face-to-face with each other and our differences. Rather than hiding behind religious jargon, Christians can and must learn new ways for practicing more open dialogue amongst ourselves. As we stand firm in freedom, corporate dysfunctions will heal. And instead of behaving as renegade misfits, we'll be forged into the family of glorious sons and daughters that we are. For truly, we will understand we are one body, and there is one God and Father over us all. (Ephesians 4:3-6)

Dreaming Big: On Mission With Jesus

Representing our Father's values is not a passive program, and we have work to do! Jesus said, "All authority in heaven and on earth has been given to Me. Go, therefore, and make disciples of all the nations, baptizing them in the name of the Father and the Son and the Holy Spirit, teaching them to follow all that I commanded you; and behold, I am with you always, to the end of the age." (Matthew 28:18-20) Therefore, each one of us must leap out of our comfort zones and participate with Him everyday—to bring about His purposes on the earth while we actively await His return. We are all called to dream big with God, and to reveal His love in practical ways and in His likeness. These are just a few examples. Outside of traditional church settings, we can meet for prayer walks or coffee talks. We can help others in times of need. We can host gatherings in our homes and intentionally share meals together, while connecting face-to-face and heart-to-heart.

Just because we haven't yet received all God promised or haven't yet apprehended the fulfillment of Jesus's prayer in Matthew 6, doesn't mean we aren't meant to! Truly, we are created for more than experiencing irregular moves of God that eventually fade. As we keep our eyes fixed on Him, and "press on toward the goal for the prize of the upward call of God in Christ Jesus," our consistent partnership with God will impact families, communities, and even whole cultures— until "the kingdom of the world has become *the kingdom* of our Lord and of His Christ." (Philippians 3:14, Revelation 11:15) In truth, the family of God is intended to carry His presence here on Earth in such a way that the weight of His glory rests on us like it did in the early days—and never lifts! Christians must become true *believers*. We are the very fulfillment of Jesus's prayer. And God's kingdom will come and His will will be done through us. (Matthew 6:10)

Abundance is the very life we're created to experience everyday, beginning here and now. And here we are, positioned at a critical crossroads. God is counting on us. In the same way our whole Thai team stood arm-in-arm, waist-deep, in the crystal-blue waters of the Andaman Sea—

not knowing what lay ahead for us–we took one last regenerative plunge together. So all of us are being commissioned into the deep with Jesus. To live fully free from the subtle deceptions that have hindered us and held us back from truly abiding in Him—to trust that each of us is invited, called, and even chosen—to join Him in *His* work. How will history remember us? One day we'll look back and realize that *this was our time*. He longs to do 'far more abundantly beyond all that we ask or think, according to the power that works within us!'" (Ephesians 3:20-21)

A Prayer of Blessing

"And I pray that he would unveil within you the unlimited riches of his glory and favor until supernatural strength floods your innermost being with his divine might and explosive power. Then, by constantly using your faith, the life of Christ will be released deep inside you, and the resting place of his love will become the very source and root of your life.

Then you will be empowered to discover what every holy one experiences—the great magnitude of the astonishing love of Christ in all its dimensions. How deeply intimate and far-reaching is his love! How enduring and inclusive it is! Endless love beyond measurement that transcends our understanding— this extravagant love pours into you until you are filled to overflowing with the fullness of God!

Never doubt God's mighty power to work in you and accomplish all this. He will achieve infinitely more

than your greatest request, your most unbeliev-
able dream, and exceed your wildest imagination!
He will outdo them all, for his miraculous power
constantly energizes you. Now we offer up to God
all the glorious praise that rises from every church
in every generation through Jesus Christ—and all
that will yet be manifest through time and eternity.
Amen!" (Ephesians 3:16-21 TPT)

EPILOGUE

Dear friend, now is the time for you to step into the full measure of your calling in Christ Jesus! You have heard His voice, and you will no longer be pushed or pulled by the charismatic words of any earthly man or woman as your guide. Only that which is spoken directly from the Lord to you will move you. He alone is worthy of your wholeness. He is enough, and in Him you are strong and complete. You have been called by Him, and thus empowered and commissioned by Him. He will sustain you by His very near and present help. Even throughout the desert seasons, He will provide. In fact, He will become your portion, your food, the feast set before you. Nothing will distract you from your oneness with Him.

Because you've been forged in the fire, you will not fear the dark. Since His light burns within you, you are the light of the world. Truly, you will dispel darkness in every place you set your foot. Since no shadow can remain hidden where His light shines, run to the places He put in your heart to go! Neither hesitate nor hold back. For He says, "Do not fear, for I am with you; do not be afraid, for I am your God. I will strengthen you, I will also help you, I will also uphold you with My righteous right hand." (Isaiah 41:10)

You will follow only Him, emblazoned by His passionate love. And as you move with Him and for Him, according to His fiery Presence within you, you will not fear risks. As you keep your eyes fixed on His, He will gird you up, above the waves that threaten to pull you down. As walking on water defies the laws of nature, that is what you're called to do. Because you live and move with your being in Him, no longer will you be bound to the natural laws set for man; you will live within the realm of the impossible. You have been prepared to step out and do hard things, things that are beyond you, even. Because His love has canceled all fear, you will step when He says, "step," even when you don't see the path ahead. You have trust in His character. And He who called you is faithful! He will not let you fall. And He says, "When you pass through the waters, I will be with you; and through the rivers, they will not overflow you. When you walk through the fire, you will not be scorched, nor will the flame burn you." (Isaiah 43:2)

ACKNOWLEDGEMENTS

Randy—You are my best friend and biggest supporter. Thank you for reading the chapters and offering feedback, for listening when I needed you, and for encouraging me to press on when I felt stuck. You are God's gift to me, and I love you forever.

My family—You stepped in and took on tasks—dinners, planning, prep, and clean-up duties—during the many hours I stepped out to write. Also, thanks for listening to my work and for your thoughtful critique; I appreciate each of your perspectives.

My parents—You brought me into this world and I'm eternally grateful. Thank you for always leading me to Jesus.

Niki, Lisa, and Stacey—Thank you for sharing your insights and opinions, and for offering the fun diversions from the work of writing. Love you always, girls.

Janice Riley—Thanks for believing in me when all I had was a word from God to begin the writing adventure.

Beta readers—Lee Gordon, Steph Flewelling, Kristina Flewelling, Ryan Musser, Shari Baer, Ed and Kathy Owens—Thanks for sharing your time and helping me to improve my work.

Gabler's—Thank you for generously opening your guest house when I needed quiet writing weekends away.

Steve Burris—I appreciate your deep spiritual insights.

Brian Kisner—I appreciate your faithful prayers.

Rich Brink—I appreciate your commitment to revival.

Christian Raffeto and team—God's timing was just right in leading me to you. Your expert skill and experience have not only shaped my work but have encouraged me to own my voice. Thank you for your patience throughout the process.

ABOUT THE AUTHOR

Jodi lives in south-central Pennsylvania, surrounded by a tight-knit community of family and friends (and 20 chickens). She expresses her love for Jesus daily—by praying for and encouraging others, showing hospitality, sharing wisdom through writing, and faithfully serving many—usually with a cappuccino in hand! She is an attentive wife and mother to six children, two of whom are thriving young adults.

As a child Jodi journaled, with dreams of one day becoming an author. She graduated from Asbury College (University) with a bachelor's degree in Social Work. Shortly thereafter, her young family served as church planting missionaries amongst an unreached people group in Thailand.

She desires for believers to fully embrace their God-given identity and inspires others to live abundantly everyday.

You can keep in touch with her via the web:

Facebook: www.facebook.com/jodi.goshorn.7

Instagram: @jodigoshorn

Website: jodigoshorn.com